Praise for
Facing the Ultimate Loss

"*Facing the Ultimate Loss* does an excellent job of giving the parent and the professional a tool for dealing with the loss of a child. It does a particularly good job of addressing the faith crisis that comes as a result of this untimely loss." **Pamela D. Blair, PhD, Psychotherapist, Spiritual Counselor & Personal Coach**

"I believe religious leaders, counselors, and anyone looking for a way to affirm life in the face of death will find solace and assurance in these pages." **Jesse R. DeWitt, Bishop, United Methodist Church, Retired**

"This book will be enormously meaningful to those who mourn the death of a child and to professionals, friends, and family members who might be called upon to help support them. Like all great books, this one should be read many times. Rabbi Marx and Davidson are experienced practitioners, compassionate scholars, and master teachers who powerfully convey wisdom, empathy, and understanding on every page. Their writings will encourage insights, feelings, and actions that empower readers both to cope with the death of a loved one and to affirm life." **Roger P. Weissberg, PhD, Professor of Psychology, University of Chicago; Executive Director, Collaborative for Academic, Social, and Emotional learning (CASEL)**

Facing
the
Ultimate
Loss

Coping with the
Death of a Child

CHAMPION PRESS, LTD.
FREDONIA, WISCONSIN

Cover Design by Fineman Communications

ISBN: 1891400991
LCCN: 2003110338

Manufactured in the United States of America 10 9

Facing
the
Ultimate
Loss

Coping with the
Death of a Child

Robert J. Marx, PhD
Susan Wengerhoff Davidson, MA

CHAMPION PRESS, LTD.

FREDONIA, WISCONSIN

"To David"

CONTENTS

Introduction

The English poet William Wordsworth tells of meeting an eight-year-old cottage girl and asking her how many brothers and sisters she has. "We are seven," she replies, and then reveals that two of them lie buried in the local churchyard.

> How many are you, then," said I,
> "If they two are in heaven?"
> The little maiden did reply,
> "O master, we are seven!"
>
> "But they are dead — those two are dead,
> Their spirits are in heaven!"
> 'Twas throwing words away; for still
> The little Maid would have her will,
> And said, "Nay, we are seven!"
> (William Wordsworth, "We Are Seven")

Death is a mystery and life is a miracle. Our destiny is to taste both the mystery and the miracle. Yet, we know that although we may develop the wisdom to understand this truth, experiencing it is quite another matter. We gladly, and sometimes routinely, accept the miracle. But, when one of our

9

own children is involved, we find it impossible to deal with the mystery, the tragedy, the desolation of death. Our book is an effort to help understand the meaning of life's greatest tragedy, and to return to hope.

The authors of this book came together quite by accident. Both of us had been helping parents deal with the loss of a child, and had independently come to the conclusion that these parents, and those who worked with them, needed a guide that would help them as they experienced the most painful ordeal anyone could be asked to endure.

We had heard about each other's work in the field of grief counseling, and agreed to meet and share ideas. Susan was a grief therapist whose practice had grown increasingly tenanted by parents who had lost a child. Robert was a parent who had watched his own child die many years earlier. One was a trained grief counselor. The other, a rabbi with years of experience devoted to helping parents of many faiths and races cope with their disbelief and despair.

It took only one meeting for us to decide that we would try to put on paper some of the thoughts and experiences that we felt might be helpful. But out of that one meeting came hours of working together, of reviewing the available literature, and of developing the ideas that went into this book. We have not always agreed with one another — nor is it important that we do so — but we have both deepened our insights and grown in our ability to understand just how painful and complex the loss of a child really is.

The fact that one of us actually experienced the loss, and the other had come to understand its anguish from a professional point of view, was a constant factor in our collaboration. We could, and did, accuse one another of being maudlin or pedantic, overly clinical, or unduly sentimental. But, out of our sessions together came not only an appreciation of each other's insights, but an understanding that both of our approaches lent themselves to the things we sought most—comfort for those who suffered, consolation for those who deemed themselves inconsolable, and hope for those who felt that their future held only despair.

We know that there are no easy solutions. Fathers and mothers have been trying to cope with the problem of loss for thousands of years. The Bible does not tell us how Adam and Eve dealt with the murder of their son Abel, but we do know that their tragedy was as much a part of the end of Eden as were the bitter consequences of tasting the forbidden fruit.

There is no shortage of books that deal with this painful subject. Many of them have proven to be most helpful—as helpful as a book can be at a time of tragedy. But we soon came to the conclusion that the volumes available to mourning parents often reflected the particular experiences of the author rather than an overview of the problems faced by the bereaved.

Is it possible to write such an overview? Two things make the effort difficult. First, people are different and mourn in uniquely different ways.

Second, various cultures and religious traditions wield a powerful influence upon the mourning process itself. These cultural distinctions often set parameters for mourning that are difficult to surmount. Some of these patterns inhibit parents as they seek ways to express their own unique yearning and pain. Others may facilitate the mourning process and offer extraordinary sources of comfort. Still other patterns are ambiguous. What is helpful to one person may not be helpful to others.

The frequently held religious belief that God takes each individual at the appropriate time may be comforting to those who hold this religious conviction, but it may also provoke resentment and anger among those who cannot accept a God who acts in this way. The affirmation or rejections of their own religion's teachings about death represent an important issue that grieving parents must confront sooner or later.

Early in our collaboration we discovered an interesting paradox: There are almost as many different ways of mourning as there are individuals. It is a foolish counselor who expects to set down rules or timetables for the mourning process. Having said that, it is equally true that there are identifiable shared feelings and responses that grieving parents experience. The sense of desolation, the feelings of despair, the meaninglessness of unrealistic timetables, the recognition that healing does not come easily — these are issues familiar to every grieving parent.

Just as there are an infinite variety of mourning patterns, so too there are countless ways in which this book can be read. For instance, some parents feel the need to read everything that will help them with their loss. They may want to do this as quickly as possible. But our experience has taught us that it is not always easy to concentrate at a time of great trauma. We urge these parents to read one chapter at a time, and not to be daunted by their inability to find instant answers or instant consolation.

Was our audience to be parents alone? As we began to work together, we realized that some of the time we were writing for those who were in mourning, and at other times we were focusing on those professionals who might be called upon to help. We hope that our readers will include both groups, and that our work, while proving helpful to parents, will also enable clergy, social workers, medical professionals, teachers, counselors, psychiatrists, and psychologists to understand more fully the problems and anguish that grieving parents encounter.

It has been our experience that all too often even trained clinicians and skilled members of the clergy are overwhelmed and uncomfortable when it comes to helping a bereaved parent. They know better than to say, "I know how you feel," unless, of course, they have experienced a similar loss. So often, however, they are left only with their basic instincts or the authority of their title or position as mandates for the help that they would like to offer. We hope that this work will help professionals gain insight into the complexities and uniqueness of this great tragedy.

But there are others who need to understand what it means to lose a child, and it is to them, too, that we address these chapters. Parents who have lost a child turn first to family and friends. Often, these initial contacts may prove to be a source of inestimable consolation. Yet, all too often, we hear of insensitive remarks or of uninformed responses that wound mourners at a time when they are so very vulnerable. To know some of the pain parents experience helps deepen the insight of those who share the anguish with them. As sympathetic as a brother is, as compassionate and hurt as a grandparent is, as loyal and understanding as a good friend is, even they may be astounded and helpless as they realize that this wound is not easily healed.

Above all, it is to offer hope and comfort that we have composed this volume. We want to say: We have been there. We have stood with others who have been there. Life is a miracle. Death is a mystery. There is light. There is hope.

1. Darkness: Can I ever accept the fact that my child is dead?

There is a moment in time beyond time. There is a moment in pain beyond pain. It is beyond consolation, beyond hope.

No matter the age, whether it is the smallest infant or a mature adult, the loss of a child is the most devastating blow that we, as parents, can experience. How many have stood over a dying child's bed and said, "I wish it were me?" And have meant it with all their hearts. We can handle the loss of a parent. We cannot handle the loss of a child.

There are no words to describe the feelings we have when we first confront the loss--when we actually pass from having a living child to a new time in which we now have only "living memories." How can we even write about it? Read about it? If it were a picture, there would be only darkness. If it were music, it would only be a cry of pain, or, for some, a single chord in a minor key — a chord extending beyond our ability to endure it. But the loss of a child is not a painting — it is not music. It is the color of our pain. It is the desperate cry of our emptiness. My son, my daughter is gone.

What is remarkable is that looking back on the moment immediately following the death of our child, our memories as parents are as varied as shells washed on the shore of the sea. The reactions range from feelings of utter desolation to bitter anger, from the long wail of pain to the deep silence of an inner search for meaning and understanding.

How can we understand statements as diverse as these?

"I wanted to hold her in my arms."

"Total numbness--the whole day was spent in total numbness."

"The nurse could not tell me that he was dead. I had to call over and over again to find out what happened."

"I begged her to stay, please--please."

"I wanted to hit him--I was so angry."

"Relief. I felt relief that it was over."

As varied as these sentiments are, they all represent the first memories of parents upon hearing that the life of their child had come to an end. Each one is a unique expression of a unique loss. Each one is an authentic reaction to those first moments--reactions based upon different histories and different relationships. To say that one is right and one wrong, one true and one false is to force our grief into a straitjacket that will not hold it.

The moment of loss is a moment of change of glacial dimensions. In one second we traverse the chasm that separates the world of living from the world of once living. Even the thought, "My child is no more," invokes more than a sense of sadness; it institutes an instant change of status for the parent who survives.

For some of us, it raises the question, Why survive? For others, it signals the onset of a new quest for meaning. For all of us, it marks the entry into a special land, a land that often has nightmarelike qualities, a land that few have seen, a land that takes us out of our past and puts us in a new place, a place of shadows and tears, a place where memory is more real than hope. To lose a child is to change in a way every bit as profound as bearing a child, and, in some ways, more profound. To lose a child is to enter a new world, a world where life and death combine in ways where it is sometimes impossible to separate the two.

"How old was your child when she died?" The question is invariably asked, months, even years, later. In some ways, the question is irrelevant—our children have become ageless—frozen in time as simply "my child." In the initial shock of loss, a little baby a few hours old may be mourned as deeply as the mature young man or woman who has traveled far along the path of life. Toddler or teenager, college student or professional, housewife, doctor, plumber, or motel attendant—the child at any age is simply "my child." Do the memories of shared experiences make the loss of an older child different from the loss of an infant? Surely later it does, but only later. The initial blow is equally harsh and unremitting for all parents.

The loss of a child produces a powerful impact on many aspects of our psychological life. It deepens our sense of pain. It assaults our sense of justice. It dulls our ability to respond. In addition, it is a cruel teacher. It teaches us how to suffer in the most unremitting way possible. And yet, it teaches us how to survive too.

We first met Sarah at one of our support groups. While other parents would express their rage and anger, Sarah would often burst into tears. From the very beginning she found it difficult to talk. For years she had watched her son suffer the effects of leukemia. Sarah's life had been one long series of disappointments — her marriage, her job that she had had to give up, and finally the loss of her only son.

Finally, one day, Sarah began to talk. "I can't be angry," she said. "My Jeremy is at peace. I suffered with him for so many years. I watched him grow weaker everyday. I cannot be angry. He is at peace." Like biblical King David, who put on sackcloth and ashes while his critically ill son fought for life, Sarah spent months watching her son waste away in pain. She had suffered with him, and, in a real sense, she had mourned, as her son struggled through the dark nights of his illness. Jeremy's death was surely not a relief in any ordinary sense, but it represented, to his mother, an end of anxiety, an end of her helplessness and worry, and an end to her son's pain. Could she have taken his place during those long years of illness, she would have done so. She sometimes said, she often thought, "You won't understand. I wished so often it could be me, not Jeremy. I couldn't make that happen by wishing it. I felt so helpless." And Sarah was right—not everyone did understand.

"How could you feel relief?" George railed at her. "When George Jr. died, I felt anger—anger at the doctors who treated him, anger at the hospital that neglected him. For the first time in my life I felt physically violent—I hit my hand against the door of his room." These were the words of a father who could not, who would not be reconciled to the death of his son.

So many feelings, so many conflicting thoughts. All have occurred in different people. And yet, they are not necessarily the different thoughts of different people. They may all occur in one parent. They may be part of the tidal waves that ebb and flow within us in those crushing first hours of loss. Anger and relief, disbelief and resignation, a desire to walk into the storm and a desire to be sheltered, a need to be alone and a need to be consoled—all are the feelings that crash over us in those tragic hours.

And all, too, are part of the effort to understand what we find so hard to understand: why a child of ours should die before we die. In the final analysis, we parents who have gone through the loss of a child, and who have experienced other losses as well, agree that it is the loss of our child that is by far the most painful of all life's experiences. Every loss is a loss--the words sound almost as if they are a cliché--but the death of a child brings a cosmic sense of desolation unlike anything that we have ever experienced.

At the end of the book of Genesis, an ailing Jacob calls his son to him, and recounts his life history. As he talks, he says, "As for me, when I came from Padden, Rachel died on me." What a strange way to describe the death of a wife--"Rachel died on me." Yet, those who have experienced the loss of a child will find Jacob's choice of words understandable. "She not only died," says Jacob, "she died on me." Our children have died on us. Their lives and deaths have left something on us that we can never remove, nor would ever want to remove. Upon each of us something is laid that changes our lives forever.

Jacob's response to Rachel's death can teach us an important lesson about loss. There are two aspects of mourning which become intensified when a child has died: the loss of the child himself, and the loss within us. The birth of a child transforms our lives. Someone incredibly wonderful was given to us. Now, that someone has been taken from us. We mourn for that beautiful spirit. We mourn, too, because of the emptiness that is now a permanent part of our lives. We cannot mourn for what we never knew — but now our pain is multiplied because of what we have known. This is the loss that becomes an eternal part of us, an indelible addition to our lives.

It is all too easy to say when someone we love passes away, that "a little bit of us has died, too."

When a child dies, this dual loss becomes even more poignant. Someone we loved very much has been stolen from us. But that is not all. Something of us, a vital part of us, has been irrevocably torn away from us, too.

We who have experienced the death of a child feel that part of our future has been ruined. What has been destroyed has to do with plans and dreams. When our child dies, part of our future seems to die, too. How can we look forward to tomorrow? How can we go to that family reunion, that Thanksgiving dinner, that high school graduation? All plans for the future are darkened by memories.

Not only is the future reordered, but the past, as well. We cannot look forward to the future. We cannot view the past in the same way we once did. The death not only affects our ability to enjoy and to find fulfillment, but it also compels us to restructure our memories, clothing the past in a cloud that is often hard to penetrate. What is destroyed is not merely an expectation of a predictable future, but a relationship that involves us in the most intimate and intricate way. It transforms the past, even as it prevents us from going forward to the future. Happy memories become bittersweet. Sad memories become beautiful. Beautiful memories become painful. Everything becomes lovely and painful at the same time. Everything becomes tears and memories. And these tears do not stop, not for a long time.

Is it better to cry? It is cathartic to cry. Giving vent

to our feelings allows us to begin to face them. But, not all people can cry. Some are too numb to cry. Some are not allowed to do so. Here is Philip's story. Philip was a successful attorney, recognized for his work in patent law. He prided himself on his ability to remain calm in the face of any crisis. He received a call at his office: "Hurry to the hospital. Your son has been hurt." Philip rushed to the hospital, and his worst fears were realized. The hospital administrator who had called had waited to give him the terrible news in person. Mark had been in a car accident and had died. Paralyzed with shock, Philip stood alone in a hospital corridor. Slowly, the reality sank in: a hit-and-run driver had killed his only son. He stood in the hall and put his hands up to his face and he began to cry. Just then a stranger passed by and saw the tears. "Be brave," he said. "Be a man. Don't cry."

In the name of false bravery that was truly cowardice, Philip had been stifled in his moment of pain. For years he could not cry. "Be a man," the words echoed in his head, "Don't cry." And only now, when he could tell the story to others, did the tears begin to slowly roll down his cheeks. He began to sob uncontrollably, comfortable at last in the presence of a group that would understand his pain. Those nearest to him gently touched his hand, put an understanding arm around his shoulders. Philip had needed to cry — had so often tried unsuccessfully to force himself to cry. For how many years was that cry stifled!

For some, indeed, it is an act of courage to cry. But,

some of us find ourselves incapable of shedding tears. Mourning turns us inward. For those who find it impossible to surrender to emotions, crying is neither an act of courage or of temerity, it is merely an impossibility. Some things are so painful that they defy external expression. Some things are so painful that we can only close our eyes and hearts and remain silent. For these people, crying would be a blessed release from the prison house in which they have placed themselves. But the tears will not come. "Cry!" friends tell us, "Let it all out, and you will feel better."

We do not cry on command, but we know that if we can voice our anguish, if we can put into tangible expression our thoughts of loss, we will have begun to recognize the chasm we must traverse. To recognize our agony is, in itself, a triumph of sorts. We can feel — even in the midst of our agony — we can feel something. We can be in touch with our own pain. To open ourselves to the inexpressible is to begin the long journey toward restoration.

Where will that journey take us? When we lose a child, we feel that our destination is uncertain. We do not know where we are going. We do not know where we want to go. We often feel, in those early days of loss, that we are being carried along by forces that are simultaneously outside ourselves and within ourselves, forces over which we have no control.

Where will the journey take us? Surely, not back to where we were before our loss. We can never return, nor, in a way, do we want to return, for we would have to return without our child. One simple thing that makes the loss of a son or daughter so very painful is that, as much as we want to return to wholeness, as much as we want to return to happiness, we never *really* want to return. If this sounds paradoxical, it is nonetheless understandable.

For to be entirely whole again would involve forgetting. To be happy again, we would need to be able to forget our pain and our emptiness. But we never want to forget our son, our daughter; therefore, we can never be whole again in the same way, or happy, as we once knew the meaning of happiness.

It is a new life that parents who lose a child must create, a life that is emptied of so much of its meaning, but, a new life nonetheless. We need to determine whether the new life into which we have been plunged has real meaning or is a life sentence in a prison that has no bars, but offers no hope of escape either.

The answer to this question lies very much in our own hands. There is help, and surely the journey is not a hopeless one. This book aims to help parents who have experienced so much sadness, understand that there are ways of facing the pain that lead to a place where life can have new meaning and value. There are wise voices to be heard — the voices of the philosophers and sages whose wisdom persists throughout the centuries, and the voices of those who have been in the place where we are now. We may be damaged, but we will not be destroyed. The path is not an easy one, but it is one we can, and should, travel. And, if we are willing to take the journey, the destination may not be a return to Eden, but perhaps to a new garden where our compassion, our understanding, and our love will grow and flourish.

2. Who Am I Now?

We change. That is the nature of life. We grow, we achieve new insights, we learn. We expect to make mistakes, and to be able to learn from them. Life may not always be fair, but it is generally reasonable.

When we lose a child, all of this changes. There is no reasonable; there is no rational. Everything we have been lead to believe about fairness and predictability vanishes in a second, and we are left standing mutely with our own shattered lives in our hands, not knowing what to do with the mess we feel we have become, not even having the strength to look at what is left of us.

We need to understand the traumatic changes that take place within us as parents, because healing can only come through acknowledging and facing the shattering changes. These are not ordinary changes.

These are changes that affect not only our future, but our view of the past as well. Life will never be the same. To face this fact, as well as the consequences, is crucial. We need to recognize the uniqueness of our experience in order to move forward with our lives. By acknowledging our feelings, we can begin to assimilate the real changes that are occurring in our lives.

William was the picture of health. He was tall and thin, and his sunburned face gave evidence of a man who loved the outdoors. William wanted to tell his story. Years ago while skiing in Utah, he fell on a difficult hill and broke his leg. As he lay on the ground, writhing in pain, he remembers thinking, "Let me go back a few minutes; let me start that run all over again. Let me do it right. Let me go back." He used to remember his skiing accident. But now these thoughts, magnified a thousand times, were attached to his daughter. William's daughter, Jill died in a terrible accident. She and her friends had been driving home on a rural road after a fraternity party, and were hit by a train at an unmarked railroad crossing. In the middle of the night, William awakens and thinks of his daughter's tragic death. When it first happened, he would think, "Let me re-write history. Let me go back a few minutes, a few days." Gradually, it became "a few months"; now, "a few years."

The death of a child changes our lives more dramatically, more traumatically than anyone who has not experienced the loss can possibly imagine. It is not simply that where there used to be a child, there is now only memory. Nor is it that the loss itself is so unbearably difficult to endure. It is that in every objective and subjective way, we become a different being, a transformed person. Life will never be the same.

There may be permanent impairment. There may be total denial. There may be serene resignation. There may be a whole gamut of emotions in between. Some parents can never recover from the loss. They do not want to. They are convinced that nothing can or will ever console them. Other parents will do anything they can to avoid mentioning their dead child. They freeze when reminded of what happened. Because they cannot bear the pain, they protest by saying that they just want to get on with their lives.

But no matter how varied the reactions, the reality is that we parents have become different in a variety of ways. Different from what we were before, different in our relationships with other people, different in our ability to laugh and cry, different in the way we view the most basic things of life.

To say we are different is not to offer a value judgment. It is to begin to understand the changes that take place. It is to begin to accept ourselves, and to find the new direction our lives will take.

Is there a "healthy" way to respond to the death of a child? Even the word "healthy" becomes suspect. "Healthy" implies something that can be measured, something that can be held up against "unhealthy" and found to be preferable. But no such standard is applicable here.

What makes the loss of a child so impossibly difficult is that most parents do not really want to stop mourning. Rather, we want to stop the pain of mourning. There is a fear that if we stop mourning, we will forget. The reality is that we never want to forget. "I will never, ever feel better. I can never forget Jody."

Isn't the fear of forgetting true of other losses as well? Aren't there loving wives who never want to forget their husbands, and dedicated children who never want to lose the memory of their parents? Surely, every one we love is part of our treasured memories. But there is a difference. When we lose a child, the very foundation of our values seems threatened. It may seem as if all meaning has been sapped from our lives. When we lose a husband or wife, we often find strands of comfort. We may hope to find someone else, or we may find consolation in children or friends. This consolation is harder to find for bereaved parents. Of course, countless men and women who remain single after losing a beloved mate indicate that there are no simple comforts. Yet, anyone who has gone through both losses will testify that there are factors in the remembering process that make the loss of a child uniquely debilitating.

"When we lose a parent, we lose the past. When we lose a child, we lose the future." Parents often express this conviction as they try to analyze why they feel so uniquely different after losing a child. And they do feel different--different than after any other tragedy or separation.

There are reasons for these differences and it will help to understand them:

1. *The length of the mourning.* The pain from other losses may be just as intense, but the pain from the loss of a child seems interminable. You cannot predict when the pain will abate, and it is not even useful to try to do so. Like most grief, there can be no timetable for mourning a child. Parents sometimes set a schedule for themselves. It does not work. "In six months I ought to feel better," or, "By the first of the year I want to be able to enjoy my old friends." These scheduled plans are doomed to frustration. In fact, they are often counterproductive. The mere establishment of a time schedule sets up a roadblock--a roadblock that only reminds us of how shattered our lives are. It also adds to our frustration and anxiety when our scheduled recovery cannot be realized.

Parents need to allow themselves time to mourn. Often time stretches far beyond their expectation. We may say, "I thought I would feel better by now," or, "If someone had told me at the beginning that the pain would last so long, I never would have believed it." It is annoying when friends and business associates ask, "Aren't you over that yet?" But, in a much more subtle way, we ask the same question of ourselves, "Why aren't we over it yet?" We cannot be over it. We don't want to be over it. To be "over it" contains elements of disloyalty to the very memories we hold most sacred. The conflict itself is part of the problem.

And so, the mourning period goes on. Grief establishes its own schedule, which no amount of planning or exhortation on our part can alter. In our mourning, our friends and family perceive the changes taking place within us, as do we.

Jan sat in the midst of mourning parents. Her adult daughter, Karen, had recently died of Crohn's Disease. The tragedy for Jan was that the disease could have been treated, but it had not been treated adequately. Much more could have been tried, such as going for consultations or getting second opinions as Jan would have wanted, but Karen's treatment had been limited by insurance constraints. Since Karen was a married adult, living with her own family out of town, Jan was not in control of the decisions that were made. Jan was sad, but she was angry, too. "I don't even recognize myself anymore. I don't care about my friends, and I don't want to hear about their children. I was never like this before!"

There are changes that trouble and anger us. But sometimes they deepen and sensitize us. The question we confront in the midst of our tragedy is: Can we be in charge of the changes that will occur in our lives? Will we allow our tragedy to make us callous and indifferent to others, or can we move in the direction of greater empathy and compassion?

2.*The loss of a future involves the shattering of hope.*
Doesn't any loss involve the shattering of hope? How
is the loss of a future with a child different from the
future we expect to have with others we love so
dearly? One answer is that every fiber of our
personality is bound up with expectations we have for
our child. We have helped create these expectations.
Not only do we love our child, but also, our whole
identity is involved in the blossoming human being
that has come from our own bodies.

When our child is born, we look down at that little
infant and begin to plan for the future. Even a newly
adopted child quickly becomes part of our hopes.
Every parent is a part of that future. One of the most
beautiful songs in the musical *Carousel* describes the
reactions of a young man named Bill who learns that
his wife is pregnant. He dreams in song about the
future son who will be named after him. He dreams
about all of the things they will do together. At the end
of the dream, he suddenly faces the "shocking reality"
that the son may be a daughter!

A shocking reality? Bill doesn't know what reality
is. He cannot know because his child is merely a
fantasy, a far cry from the boy or girl who actually
lives and grows, laughs and cries. To have it all come
to an end — that is the starkest reality of all. What
future can there be? The road home involves the slow,
sometimes painfully slow realization that there is still a
future — there is hope.

3. *There is a biological factor in the loss of a child.* The loss of a child, in a very real sense, involves a loss of a physical part of ourselves. We may feel other losses with equal emotional pain. Surely we lose a sense of the future, whether it is a spouse or a child who has died, but only our child is a part of us, a physical, biological part of us. "Flesh of my flesh, bone of my bone," my child is a living extension of me.

The loss of a child, then, is so transforming because it represents not only the death of another person who is precious and beloved, but also, the death of a part of ourselves. We may feel as if a vital part of our own life has been stolen away. Jan was struggling with these feelings when she described her loss as an amputation; "a living part of my body has died." This mother was merely trying to invoke a physical description to understand how our emotional ties to someone we love can lead us to respond in physical and emotional ways. It is no mere coincidence that after a painful loss a survivor may actually encounter a serious illness. The feeling that "Something I created is gone," transforms to "Some part of me is gone."

4. *"You become a little crazy."* The changes that occur when we lose a child not only affect our attitudes and moods, but can cause deep changes in our personalities. One day, Sarah put it in the starkest terms: "I have become a little bit crazy." The actual words have been used by more than one parent, and,

they echo the sentiments that so many feel. Life is never the same. "I cannot laugh in the same way. I cannot cry in the same way. It is all different."

What is the meaning of this sense of craziness? Part of it has to do with our understanding of a rational life. Reason instructs us that older people should die before younger ones, parents before children. A child dies. Reason has been stood on its head.

Another part stems from a sense that we are now different from other people—from "normal people." What seems so important to them may seem trivial to us. We see things from a different perspective. It is not only our lives that have changed, it is the meaning of life. Nowhere is this more vividly illustrated than in a story Julie told about the death of her teenage daughter. Elizabeth had become a skilled horseback rider. One Friday afternoon, she was riding in an indoor stable and was thrown from her horse. She was unconscious. Rushed to the hospital, the doctors assured Julie that Elizabeth had suffered nothing more than a concussion. Two days later she was dead. "I lied to her," Julie sobbed, "I told her she would be all right. I knew she would be all right." Not only did Julie lose her child, but, her whole sense of integrity. For years, her life had been on hold while she tried to forgive herself for having "lied" to her daughter.

People change in profound ways. Some of us become impatient with things that we used to take for granted. We become impatient with unimportant things that seem to be overvalued by others. Some of us may change in the opposite direction and become remarkably more serene. In the midst of a family reunion, we may suddenly become wistful and morose. Or, we may develop a sense of black humor. Absurd and bizarre situations may begin to strike us as humorous.

The changes that parents experience are both subtle and profound. For many, these changes have to do with moods. "I never used to get angry easily," George said, "and now I jump at the slightest provocation." Sometimes these angers are misplaced and even inappropriate. But, whether misplaced or not, they are often close to the surface, and easily aroused. "I know this is wrong, but I can't help it," Barbara said. "I am furious at my son-in-law. Why? He is here and my daughter is not. She will never be here again. I am furious at God. How could He do this to me?"

We shall study these angers more fully in Chapter Nine, but it is important to understand now that angry feelings are more than merely reactions to the tragedy itself. They may become more or less permanent features of a life that can no longer endure the ordinary routines of life, and that has been transformed by suffering.

Guilt, anger, and sadness are all characteristics of the transforming process. They are often accompanied by changes in attitudes toward situations that arise in everyday life, changes that may occur suddenly or over a long period of time. "When the men in my office start to talk about the Sunday football games, I get up and leave. They act like this is life or death. It is all so trivial. I think of George Jr. and I just have to get out of there."

It is not unusual to change friends following a loss. The people we once knew and loved may suddenly become reminders of what we have lost.

Andrew was an overworked tax accountant. Like George, he loved the outdoors. The two men found a common bond in their love for fishing and skiing. But Andrew found it impossible to go back to the outdoors he had once loved. "I find it more comforting to read the letters my friends sent me than to see them," Andrew admitted one day. "I find it easier to go to my office than to spend time with friends who remind me of the annual fishing trips we all took together when Charlie was alive."

Paradoxically, but equally discernible, are those parents who become upset at the refusal of friends to talk about their dead child. "I don't want him to become a non-person," said George. "I don't want them to pretend he didn't exist. George Jr. had a life, and you just can't erase him!" The need to forget and to remember is part of the same pattern—a pattern in which pain and memory mingle in a continuous, never-ending conflict.

Values change, too, even values involving life and death issues. Even fear of death may lose its terror, and illness may be greeted with a new sense of equanimity. Parents nodded vigorously in agreement when a member of their support group told them: "Three months ago, I had major surgery. For the first time in my life, I didn't care about the pain. I didn't even care whether I lived. All I could think about was my Karen." For so many parents, the fear of their own death loses its sting. They have already gone through the valley of the shadow. What greater terror can there be?

There is yet another pitfall that grieving parents need to recognize. That is the pitfall of lethargy, or laziness. It is not unusual to feel tired or listless after losing a child. Things that "normal" parents take for granted may become chores for bereaved parents. Even the simple task of getting up in the morning may seem a terrible burden.

When these feelings are carried to extremes, they can lead to indifference toward life itself. In its most extreme manifestations, this life-weariness can even lead to thoughts of suicide. "I have set before you life and death, the blessing and the curse; therefore chose life, that you may live. (Deut. 30:19) " The fulfillment of this biblical commandment is not an easy one. Surely, it is not easy for parents who have lost a child. Yet, we need to find the strength and the will to endure. It is so important for parents to realize that the challenge to meet life anew is a critical part of their journey toward wholeness.

We need to realize, though the yoke seems too painful to bear, that there are beautiful possibilities in our suffering. There are hidden blessings too, as we are yet to see, blessings that may touch the lives of each of us. It is these blessings that we must come to understand and appreciate. But this takes time—often, a long time. They are blessings that a newly bereaved parent will not, cannot, yet understand. They may be recognized only after a long dark night of mourning eases into the glimmer of dawn. They are blessings that are tinged with pain and bitterness, and yet, are all the more beautiful because they have been earned slowly and honestly.

It is true that parents who have lost a child see things differently. Surely this is not always a negative. Parents may become more thoughtful and introspective, more patient and sympathetic. They can feel the joy and sadness of others in new and deepened ways. And sometimes, with time and effort, these new insights lead not to a life of despair, but to one that has new and unexpected possibilities.

3. How Can We Ever Say Goodbye? Ceremonies of Separation

Every society, every religion has its way of coping with death. Our children will remain with us forever in our thoughts and our love. There is no way we can keep our children physically with us; but it is so impossibly difficult to let go. The funeral is a painful bridge between the moment of death and the long days of mourning that follow it.

A funeral may last only a few minutes or a few hours, but memories of the funeral remain with us, and often frame the weeks and months of mourning that follow. The funeral takes place at a moment in time, but there is something timeless about it. We are compelled to think about it in the hours immediately following our loss. But we think about it, too, years afterward. Memories of who was there and what was said may remain vividly in our minds. Conversely, we may be so numb that we remember none of the details, except the efforts of those around trying to console us.

And those who console us may also surprise us. We expect old friends to be at our sides, and often they are there in heroic fashion. But sometimes they disappoint us. This absence may have little to do with their love for us or for our child. Their own fears and pain may be too terrifying; their anxiety too intense; their sense of inadequacy too overwhelming. They have let us down.

But conversely, we often find strength from new and unexpected sources. Someone who had only been peripherally involved in our lives becomes the rock of our support—willing to step in when others disappoint us. We do not know what gives someone the strength to help us during these painful days, but we are grateful for those willing to assume the burden that we are unable to shoulder alone.

Funerals fulfill several important functions. Besides being a bridge between life and death, they are a ritualistic acknowledgment that a precious life has come to an end. Funerals also provide a way for other people, family as well as strangers, to deal with their own sense of shock, sadness and loss. They offer our family and friends a way of reaching out and helping.

Every religion and every society has its own way of coping with death and its own way of helping those who mourn. We may think that we are dealing with a funeral only at the time of our loss. Actually, we deal with it long afterward. Whether it is a mass or a *minyan,* a service held within a few hours of death or one postponed for days, an interment in the ground or a cremation, the choices we make, or that are made for us, haunt our thoughts for many years to come. We cannot always make the decisions that have to be made at the time of such intense suffering. "I was so grief stricken, I could not make up my mind about a single detail of the funeral," said Marie. But, not everyone feels that way. "Everyone tried to tell us what to do," Pam and Stuart said, "but, she was *our* baby and we wanted to do it *our* way." Truly, we all react differently to the crises of our lives. Some of us can respond instinctively; we want to deal with every detail of the funeral process. Others are grateful when they can leave these painful decisions to family or friends. Some are too stunned to even care, too shattered to act.

The funeral is an act shaped by society. Its words and rituals are determined by the traditions to which we belong. Its rites are fashioned by centuries of history. Many people find these traditions helpful and comforting—they have stood the test of time. We are individuals, though, and may not wish to be bound by the past; we react differently and need to hear different things when we suffer so painfully. It is not unusual for parents to feel that rituals designed for mourners in general do not fit the specific needs of parents who lose children. "Walk through the valley of the shadow of death," Sarah said, "my child could not walk!" "We spend our years as a tale that is told," Pam and Stuart said, "but Peter's tale was never told!" For these parents, the designing and fashioning of the service may, in itself, be an act of supreme dedication.

The Nobel-prize-winning writer Rabindranath Tagore used to tell the story of a household in India where the head of the house berated his maid servant for having come in late to work. "What shall I do with you," he lamented. "This is the third time this month that you have been late to work. I expect punctuality from my employees." The maid swept the floor. "I buried my daughter this morning," she said. And kept on sweeping.

For some, tears and friends provide the wire that holds them together. For others, the need for privacy proves all consuming. And, of course, the two moods may mingle and replace one another like the ebb and flow of the tide.

When the son of Rabbi Yohanan ben Zakkai died, the master's disciples came to console him. First came Rabbi Eliezer ben Hyrkanos. Wishing to distract the bereaved father, he asked, "Would you like me to comfort you, Rabbi?" "Speak!" Rabbi Yohanan assented. So, Rabbi Eliezer began: "Adam had a son and he died. Nevertheless, Adam allowed himself to be comforted. We construe this from the fact that Adam and Eve reconciled themselves to their loss and fulfilled their allotted tasks on earth. So, you, too, Master, must find solace in your bereavement."

"It is not enough that I have my own sorrows," cried Rabbi Yohanan reproachfully, "must you remind me of the sorrows of Adam?"

Rabbi Joshua then entered and said, "Will you allow me, Rabbi, to try to comfort you?" "Speak," said Rabbi Yohanan. Rabbi Joshua began: "Job had sons and daughters, but, they all died in one day. Nevertheless, he found solace. How do we know that? From the fact that he said: 'God gave and God took, blessed be the name of the Lord!' You, too, must find comfort."

"It is not enough that I have my own grief, must you remind me of Job's grief?" Rabbi Yohanan cried reproachfully.

The last to go in to him was Rabbi Eleazar ben Arak. "Will you allow me, Rabbi, to say words of comfort to you?" he asked.

"Speak," said Rabbi Yohanan. Rabbi Eleazar began: "Let me tell you a fitting parable. A king had given one of his vassals a valuable object to hold for him. Each day the man would lament: 'Woe is me! When will the king come and take back his possession so that I won't be burdened with such a great responsibility?' The same holds true of you, Rabbi. You had a son who was accomplished and a fine scholar. He left the world unstained, pure from sin. Therefore, you must find comfort in the thought that you have returned unsullied the possession entrusted in your care by the King of Kings."

"You have comforted me, Eleazar, my son!" cried Yohanan. And he arose and put grief aside. (Quoted from Nathan Ausubel, *A Treasury of Jewish Folklore*, p. 111f, Adapted from the Agada in the Talmud — Consolation in Grief)

Rabbi Yohanan was comforted by the assurance that his child had returned to God. Can all parents believe this way? Do they want to believe it? For some, surely, the assurance of an eternal life with God is a source of tremendous comfort. But just as assuredly, other parents will question the justice of a God who could give so lightly and take away with such a crushing blow someone they loved so much.

The funeral provides an essential bridge between life and death. Beyond the words, beyond the rites, the funeral has a function, which, when understood, can lead to healing and consolation. That function is to unite life with death, individuals with community, despair with hope.

In terms of uniting life with death, the funeral service of most faiths, when it is properly understood, serves to promise that death is not the end of human existence. Over the centuries there have been a variety of answers to the question, What happens after I die? Not only do religious traditions offer different answers, but also, even within the major faiths themselves, different branches or movements may offer divergent approaches. Answers within these traditions range from an outright dismissal of any belief in the hereafter to assurances of a bodily as well as a spiritual resurrection.

Buddhists, who believe in the transmigration of souls, pray for a release of the soul from the cycle of death and rebirth. To escape from the wheel of Karma is the goal of the devout. Religions in the Jewish, Christian, and Muslim traditions believe in varying forms of afterlife, including a physical place where the righteous dwell as well as a place of eternal damnation. Most, though not all, Christians believe that the Messiah has manifested himself, and will return again, bringing redemption and renewed life to those who have died. Traditional Jews believe that the Messiah has not yet arrived, and they couple a belief in the immortality of the soul with a belief that a bodily resurrection will occur when the Messiah does arrive.

Any one of these beliefs may be expressed during the funeral rites and remain as part of a spiritual support system for those who mourn. Each of them serves to unite the living with the dead in tangible ways. Even those traditions that emphasize life in this world rather than in a world to come, speak of ways in which those we love live on—in memory, in their good deeds, if not in more mystical ways.

Death is not the end—to express this is the function of the funeral. This is the message of the funeral that sustains mourners even years after the rite itself has been performed.

The funeral unites individuals with the community. Family and friends join in the act of mourning. The suffering parent is not alone. A whole religious history is present at the ceremony. Centuries-old traditions of dealing with death are also invoked in order to console and comfort.

Parents understand that the act of integrating life with death is not easy to achieve. Not only may the ceremony sometimes seem cold and irrelevant, but the person responsible for conducting the funeral may be a source of disappointment. A minister or priest or rabbi who has not personally experienced the death of a child may well feel intimidated by the awesome task that has been placed on his or her shoulders. It is indeed an overwhelming responsibility to try to offer consolation in such foreign territory. Clerics who pride themselves on their familiarity with a wide variety of spiritual crises cannot claim knowledge in this dark terrain. They cannot know how these parents feel, and to presume that they do is to invite a crisis of confidence.

But the role of the clergy can be a vital source of comfort. Religious leaders officiating at the funeral of a child need to understand how truly helpful they can be. They can be buttressed with an understanding that their presence can help restore the unity between the parents and their community. To connect parents and child is one role. To connect parents and community is quite another. Both opportunities are present at the funeral.

Parents often point out that around the time of the funeral, friends seem to change. The death of a child is a frightening event. Friends want to help, but they cannot find the words; they cannot fathom the acts that will truly comfort. Some of their problem is awkwardness. They just do not know what to do. But there is another dimension to the problem. Friends can be afraid. They can be afraid to face so much sadness. They can be afraid that the tragedy they see unfolding before them might reach out and touch them too. The loss of a child is such an unnatural event, that it requires courage to confront it—courage for those not related, as well as courage for the immediate family. How many mourning parents have reached out a hand to a disconsolate friend or hugged a distraught acquaintance? The mourner can become the comforter. It happens frequently enough to merit our attention and understanding.

The funeral unites despair with hope. It is too simple to see the funeral as merely an expression of despair or mourning. The funeral carries a message that might well be re-enacted long after the ceremony ends. My son, my daughter is gone. But, there is much that remains. It is more than memory. It is more than nostalgia. It is the possibility of creating something lasting and beautiful, something that preserves the memory and sanctifies it.

The funeral sets the tone for such acts of consecration. Many parents complain that too many traditional funerals seem to be written for someone who has lived a long and creative life. What does the liturgy say for someone who lived only a few days, or a few years? What does the liturgy say for a young college student snatched away in the prime of life? Or, more difficult, what does it offer to the parents of a teenager who took her own life?

While some religions insist on a traditional ritual, others encourage parents to join in the preparation of the liturgy. "We all went down to the river's edge," Barbara remembered. "All of Janie's friends were there. We sat at the river she loved so much. We made little boats of paper and placed candles in them. As it became dark, we lit the candles and set them all a sail. Seventy candles floated down the river. Janie was with us."

Here is a family that concluded the funeral with a picnic. "Gil would have wanted it that way," said Brian. Brian was a retired television repairman. He loved to fix things. The only thing he couldn't fix was the grief he and his wife, Ilene, both felt when their son died of acute pancreatitis. "Every year since he died, we have held a picnic and served all the foods Gil liked. He would have loved being remembered that way."

A funeral is a way of connecting the past to the future. To personalize it, to move beyond tradition into something that has symbolic meaning for the families, is to allow time to stand still and to recreate itself in memories that live.

We who have lost a child dread certain moments and certain experiences. Among the most dreaded is the anniversary of the loss. The date seems to cast a cloud over the days and even weeks which precede it. The anniversary is coming. The anticipation produces an ominous sense of doom. It can seem as if the tragedy is about to occur again. That the anticipation is often more dreadful than the day itself may be typical, but hardly reassures us who have come to expect the storm clouds to gather, and watch them come in as an annual visitor—a visitor whose presence is always unwelcome, yet always expected.

Our society increasingly distances us from death. Our elderly are placed in nursing homes or in retirement communities—not all, but, increasingly larger numbers of them. In a former time, it was regarded as a blessed responsibility to care for the sick and dying. Now, with changed economic conditions and our growing alienation from death, we find it a difficult subject to confront. We hire others to do this for us. It is professionals that care for the sick, hospitals and nursing homes that house them. We have removed ourselves from the awful/beautiful opportunity to wash the dying, to change their bedclothes, to fix their meals. That task is relegated to others—most often, to strangers.

Unfortunately, our society has increasingly moved to depersonalize the rituals that help us to confront death. The modern cemetery is merely a symbol of this depersonalization. Even its location affects parents in the days and years following the funeral.

Our growing alienation from death affects the places where we put our dear ones at the end of their lives. One hundred fifty years ago, cemeteries were in the center of town. The old churchyards or the village squares still bear the memorials to a time when our dead were to be kept near us. Now, our zoning laws, and our social attitudes relegate most cemeteries to distant suburban areas, or to parts of the city where "cemeteries belong." " The cost of land makes this necessary," said one real estate man. But the "cost of land" is related to the social importance of land, and the building of cemeteries is less important in our times than the building of high-rise office buildings, or high cost sports arenas.

Unlike in earlier times, few parents visit the grave of their child daily. As a matter of fact, many parents are ambivalent about whether to visit the grave of their child at all. Not only is the cemetery so far away, but the visit itself is a reminder of the whole tragedy that has befallen their family. "I cannot visit," Philip complained. Ever since his son Mark's car accident, Philip had a problem with cemeteries. "I want to go, but I cannot stand at Mark's grave. It is too difficult for me." Everyone knew that Sarah went to the cemetery every week since Jeremy died of leukemia. "I go every week," said Sarah. "Nothing comforts me more."

These are but two of the attitudes that assail parents who have lost children. Is one healthy and one abnormal? The world of the mourning parent is a world where health and normality are terms that can be used only with extreme caution. That we must listen to our own inner voices is wise advice to those plunged in sadness. And those voices echo differently within each of us. The final words of Shakespeare's King Lear comprehend both the pain and the promise of this possibility: "The weight of this sad time we must obey. Speak what we feel, not what we ought to say!" (King Lear, Act V, Scene III).

4. *Fingerprints in Time*

E very grief is as individual as a fingerprint. How is it possible to describe grief? It is a different experience for everyone.

You are asleep in your warm, comfortable bed. Suddenly, a large bird swoops down and picks you up. It carries you off. It drops you. When you hit the ground, you are aware of experiencing incredible pain – pain that you have never felt before. You are terrified. You have absolutely no idea where you are or what you are doing there. You see people coming toward you. You feel relieved. Perhaps they will be able to help you. You soon discover that many of them speak a foreign language, some are afraid to speak to you, and others are no help because they don't know where you have come from or where you are trying to go. You are in so much pain that you can barely think. You are afraid. You realize you are alone, and, in your aloneness, realize

*that if you are to escape, you will have to do it yourself. And
so you start.*

*You realize that you don't know where you are, and you
don't know where to go, but you know you don't want to
stay where you are. So, you start the long journey home.
Along the way, if you are lucky, you meet a few people who
are willing to help. They listen to you describe the place you
came from, but, they cannot speak, and then, some of them
try to speak, but their words are meaningless.*

Grief is a world in which we speak a language
unique to ourselves. Grief is a world in which we are
thrown to the ground, and do not know how to get up.
It is a world in which even those who try to help us
seem to be speaking a foreign language, or no
language at all. It is a world in which we feel so alone,
so devastated, that even those closest to us sometimes
cannot understand or help us.

The problem with grief is not only the unbearable
burden of pain which characterizes it, but the
unpredictability. When you go to the dentist, you
know what to expect — the pain of the drill will last
fifteen or twenty minutes. But our grief is unbounded
by time. It is an ache that comes and goes, and the fact
that our pain is deep within the recesses of our
consciousness makes it inacessible. Even the most
skilled surgeon cannot excise it. Grief is an infection,
not of the body — but, of the soul.

Grief is like being thrown to the ground over and over again. You try to get up. You feel you are getting up. And all of a sudden, you find yourself slammed into the ground once again. You know you ought to be used to the pain. You feel it ought to end. But it just goes on and on. Some days are easier than others. Some days you don't even take a single step. Other days you feel that you have made progress. And other days you have to go back and retrace your steps.

"I didn't want to get up this morning. I couldn't face the day. I wanted to come to this parents' meeting, and that is the only thing that got me started. But it is no use. My life is of no use to anybody." That's what Jan said, as she struggled to understand how she could feel better one day and so utterly devastated the next.

Barbara reached over to her and gently took her hand. Barbara usually found it difficult to think about anyone else, but today she seemed to be assuming a new and transformed role. For some reason, Jan's anguish touched her very deeply. "I know the feeling. There are some days that I can have lunch with friends. I did that yesterday. I felt so happy. I even laughed a couple of times. And then I went home and thought of Janie and started to cry."

There is no pattern—no rational way to understand these attacks of grief. Sometimes they take the form of an anguished cry of desperation, and other times they are swallowed up by an inability to give voice to anything at all. And now it was Andrew's turn to speak. He stuttered slightly, but his thoughts were clear. "When I think of Charlie I just don't want to talk to anybody. I don't want to be with anybody. I just want to get in my car and drive." Andrew used his car as a means of isolating himself from people and feelings.

Wouldn't it be nice if there were a grief map and timetable? You could follow along and chart your progress, compare yourself to others who had experienced losing a loved one. If you were in a particular stage or mood, you could merely consult the timetable to see how long you would probably stay in that phase. Unfortunately, we all know that life is not that simple. There are no maps for those who grieve; grieving parents must create their own emotional maps. Each loss represents uncharted territory.

We express emotions in a wide variety of ways. Watch any group of people engaged in an activity, and you will observe a wide gamut of reactions. At a sporting event, some observers will be cheering, some screaming, some passively watching, and some will be talking to others, unaware of what is going on during the game. Similarly, grief responses vary tremendously from person to person. Some of us are outwardly emotional and feel a need to express our feelings through talking and crying. Some of us may not wish to display our feelings and may try not to let our feelings show outwardly. Some may want the company of others, while others refuse company. Some people may scream, while others retreat into a shell and choose to be quiet with their own thoughts.

How amazing is the great variety of emotions that we all feel and the different ways in which we express them.

What is felt during grief are feelings so new and foreign that there is no way to predict them. A person who has been soft-spoken and mild-mannered all his life may not remain so when faced with a tremendous loss. The loss of a child is so traumatic that few of us remain as we were before the loss. Changes occur that could never have been anticipated.

Religious convictions, as we have noted, affect not only our view of life and death, but they can also touch us as we face our sadness. Traditional religious convictions can support someone who has lost a child in vital ways, but they can also, themselves, be the focus of great anguish, and even anger. To be sure, grieving parents may be consoled by religion. But at times we may feel a need to confront religion. Previously held beliefs may be questioned. Faith may be replaced by anger. "How could God do this to me?" is an often-heard cry of a mourning mother or father. Again, the pattern is not always neat and predictable. Paradoxically, someone who has not been observant may turn to religion as a source of comfort and consolation during a time of loss.

Further complicating things is the fact that people's responses to past losses may not be similar to how they react now. We remember how we responded to the death of our parent. How differently we feel when we face the death of our child.

"One Day at a Time" is one of the phrases used by Alcoholics Anonymous and many other groups that help individuals deal with their lives in small parts rather than by always looking at the whole situation. This phrase could apply to grief as well. Each day is a new day in the journey through grief.

Not only do we react differently in different grief situations, but we may react differently, too, in dealing with the same loss. At moments we cannot stop crying. In other moments, we cannot make ourselves cry. "Talk to me about Elizabeth," Julie said. And five minutes later, she said, "I can't stand this anymore. Let's talk about something else." At times our grief leads us to do nothing but remember the pleasant moments, and at times, it leads us to feel guilty about what we said, or about things left unsaid.

Our grief bears no resemblance to an escalator that continues its path upward. It is much more like a roller coaster in its continuous highs and lows. We may feel so miserable one day that getting out of bed is too difficult, yet may feel like going out to dinner or to the movies the next day. It is possible to be driving peacefully along a country highway when a thought or song or glimpse dissolves us into tears. The unpredictable nature of grief is the only thing that is predictable about it. We like things in our lives to be calm and stable, and to know what we can expect from others and ourselves. Grief leaves us only with the uneasy knowledge that more grief lurks around the corner.

There are no classes to take to learn to grieve. We often have preconceived notions about how to grieve "properly"--i.e., how long to cry, how long to mourn, how to behave in public, not to talk about the child for fear of upsetting someone, etc. Parents seeking counseling say things like, "I need you to help me stop crying", or, "I should be better by now." They also ask questions like, "When will I be better?" and "When will I stop hurting?"

We seem to want rules as to the correct way to behave. But there are no rules, and the search for them can make an already unbearable situation even more difficult. Because we have no prior experience with grief, we may set unrealistic or imaginary standards for ourselves based upon what we have seen in movies or on television, read in books, or observed in others. When President Kennedy died in 1963, Jacqueline Kennedy displayed what some consider a courageous standard for proper bereavement behavior. She remained the unflappable, stylish, brave, dignified widow as she and Caroline and John, Jr. buried their husband and father. This sent a clear, strong, and yet, a questionable message--emotions are to be kept in check. If there are to be tears, they should be shed in private. Many of us have retained that image of "correct" funeral decorum. If we cannot live up to that standard, we perceive ourselves as weak.

Many people in our automated society encourage this type of thinking. They give the bereaved a message about what they "should" be doing or how they "should" be acting. Unfortunately, this form of "comfort" is often motivated more by their own discomfort than by thoughts of what could be helpful for those who are suffering.

There is no such thing as grieving etiquette. The only "should" in grief is that we need to recognize its awesome staying power. When we set arbitrary rules or definitions for grief, we stifle its real message, and also its tremendous healing power. We will have to talk about its power later, but we need to recognize it now, for not only its pain, but also its importance.

In a counseling session, Jan talked about how she had been unable to meet her friends' expectations. She was still mourning, and, they wanted her to be over it. "I failed grief," she said.

Since guilt is often such a large part of the grief process, it is important not to add to guilt by feeling that you aren't doing it "right." Dealing with any loss makes us feel vulnerable and insecure. Dealing with the loss of a child makes us feel even more so. When we try, unsuccessfully, to reach some arbitrary or unrealistic standard, our confidence and self-esteem suffer immeasurably. We need to recognize that grief is an intensely personal, individual process. There is no right or wrong. The path through grief is a tortuous one, but it is a path which, if we follow it courageously, can lead us home to healing.

5. Do Our Children Ever Die?
A Biblical Parable

Some stories can be helpful, even when they disturb us, and that is the theme of this chapter. We have already discovered the common threads that unite most parents who have lost a child—a sense of desolation, anger and a feeling that this loss is like no other we have ever experienced. But we have seen, too, that parents may react in totally different ways to the same situation. What brings solace to some may prove annoying to others. What some find patronizing, others find comforting.

Our ancient traditions are full of legends about life and death. Many of these legends raise dilemmas in uncomfortable ways. They provide us with opportunities for both thought and discussion, allowing us to relate the timeless experiences of others to our own.

The story of the Shunamite woman is a thought-provoking story in the Book of Kings, one that raises many questions about the problems most parents experience. The Shunamite woman may arouse us to anger, or it may comfort us, depending on how we understand it. It may be useful in helping us think about some of the problems that confront all of us who have lost a child. It you want to read the entire story of the Shunamite woman, look at Second Kings, Chapter 4 (verses 8-37).

The story starts with the Bible telling us a little bit about Elisha, the prophet. Elisha was the spiritual heir of Elijah and a great man in his own right. "The word of the Lord is with him." That is how King Jehoshaphat describes this powerful religious personality. In his travels across the countryside, accompanied by his servant, Gehazi, Elisha meets an unusual woman. The Bible calls her a "great woman," but she is so great that the Bible never gives her a name. All we know about her is that she lives in a place called Shunam, is married to a much older man, and is childless. We know that she is hospitable, too. She offers Elisha a permanent room in an upper chamber of her home, and furnishes it for him--a bed, a table, a stool, and a candle.

A grateful Elisha tells his servant, Gehazi, to ask this generous lady what he can do to repay her. But, the Shunamite woman has no demand. "I dwell among my people," is her simple response. When

Gehazi reminds Elisha that the woman is childless, the great prophet announces that within a year the woman will bear a child, a son, no less.

Filled with disbelief, the Shunamite woman can only respond, "Please, do not lie to me." But, the prediction is true. A son is born to the Shunamite woman. He grows. He thrives. He helps his father in the fields. And then, one day, in a moment of agony, he calls out, "My head, my head." He is carried back to his mother--and he dies.

We can only imagine the feelings that mother experienced. The Bible doesn't say a word about her emotions, not one word, but we know what she did. She carried the child upstairs and placed him on Elisha's bed. Quickly she called one of her servants, had him saddle a donkey, and lead her to Elisha. When she saw the prophet she threw herself at Elisha's feet so forcefully that the prophet's assistant had to pull her away. But, Elisha understood that something terribly wrong had happened. "Leave her alone," he tells Gehazi, "for her soul is bitter within her."

"Did I ask you for a son?" she screams at Elisha. "Didn't I tell you not to lie to me?" And then she does something both angry and courageous. "I will not leave you," she screams, "I will not leave you alone!" The prophet knows that he just must find some way to comfort this desperate and determined lady.

And now, the story becomes a fantasy. Something that happens only in our wishes happens to the Shunamite woman. The events flash before us. We see

Elisha and Gehazi and the mother rushing back toward the child. We see the prophet's assistant racing ahead, Elisha and the Shunamite woman close on his heels, speeding toward that ill-fated home. We see them rushing up the stairs to the attic room, finding that lifeless child on the prophet's borrowed bed.

A miracle occurs. Elisha offers artificial respiration. The Bible describes the emergency scene this way: Elisha lies upon the child, "his mouth upon his mouth, his eyes upon his eyes, and his hands upon his hands," and the child opens his eyes. He is alive. He is safe. What an incredible moment, the mother bowing down to the ground in joy and disbelief, picking up her child tenderly in her arms! "And she took her son," the Bible tells us "and went out." That is the end of the story. She simply "went out."

The story of the Shunamite woman raises many issues that confront parents who have lost a child. These issues involve vital differences that occur precisely at the moment of birth and of death. They fall into a category we can only describe somewhat awkwardly as "the difference between." There is, of course, a world of difference between having a child and not having one. This is the difference that occurs at the moment of birth. There is also a world of difference between having a child who is alive and one who has passed away.

It may be a simplification, but becoming a parent changes our lives forever. No matter how much we wished for that child, we become transformed at the actual moment of birth. We are now and forever more, parents, and we can never go back to the time when we were not parents. Similarly, there is a mountainous difference between the moment when our child is still alive and the moment when death occurs. We cannot go back. Life is forever changed.

Birth and death are the two crucial events that spare no human being. We have all known couples who have desperately tried to conceive a child but have been unsuccessful. They will go to visit marriage counselors, physicians, sex therapists. For others, the pregnancy may be a rather routine event, occurring either in a planned or unexpected way. The key event, however, occurs with the actual birth of the child. Whether planned or unanticipated, the arrival of a child in the family is a magical and transforming act.

Let us look for a moment at how the story of the Shunamite woman raises some basic questions about birth as well as death. The wealthy woman of Shunam has passed the point where she even expects a child. Her husband is old, and she herself harbors no illusions about her ability to become pregnant. And, yet, suddenly, she is pregnant. "Don't lie to me," she tells Elisha. We wonder what she was really thinking. Was it too good to be true? Was she afraid of the responsibilities of parenthood? She was satisfied with her life. "I live with my people," was her simple response when Elisha originally asked her what she wanted. She could have been afraid of having a child at her age. And, now she finds herself pregnant.

The birth of her son removes whatever doubts she once had. The prophet has not lied. The son grows and flourishes. Her already full life becomes even more beautiful.

But, suddenly all that comes to a crushing end. Crying out "My head, my head," the son stops breathing, and is carried lifeless to the upper chambers, to Elisha's room. The Shunamite woman had greeted the news of her impending pregnancy with suspicion, and, even a degree of cynicism. Was this something she really wanted? Did she ask Elisha to allow her to become pregnant? What we do know is that once the child was born, she did what mothers do—she loved her child with an intensity that she had never thought imaginable.

And now, this unexpected child, this child that she has learned to love so much is dead. We can only imagine her rage—her tremendous resentment. Something dramatic happens in the story now. The Shunamite woman is determined to do what every mother wishes she could do. She is not content to remain with rage alone. This is where the story causes all of us anguish, and a sense of recognition. The Shunamite woman decides that her anger can bring back her child. We can all understand that feeling and can identify with it. If only we could create the happy ending.

The Shunamite woman was able to bring back her child. We cannot. This marks the difference between the world of parable and the world of reality. It marks the difference between life and death. It also marks the difference between feeling that something can be corrected, and facing the inevitability of our own helplessness in the face of death.

The story of the Shunamite woman may well anger parents who have lost a child. For that "great lady" seems to have achieved something that we can only desperately yearn for--the return of our child. From this point of view, the story of the miracle that Elisha wrought for the Shunamite woman may leave us angrier than relieved, more despairing than hopeful.

Grieving parents may rejoice when they learn of a child who has been saved from some great peril, but deep inside, many of us draw little comfort in our own lives from this news. Every day we read stories about how children were remarkably saved from impending disaster. A little girl is wedged in an abandoned well. Workers dig carefully for days, and, then, joyously pull the child to safety. A child caught in the currents of a stormy lake, is pulled unconscious to safety and is gradually nursed back to health. There are miracles in our world. We are pleased that someone has been saved. But, our child was not saved, and these newspaper miracles are not our miracles.

And too, we read the stories of children who have died tragically. A nine-year-old girl shot in a random drive-by shooting. A thirteen-year-old boy killed when a drunken driver crosses the median strip of a superhighway. The names of these children make the news for a day, two days, and, then they are forgotten. They are forgotten and their parents are forgotten. These parents are left bearing only the tattered shreds of their memories — as are we.

Does the story of the Shunamite mother fail to recognize the depths of a bereaved parent's anguish? Paradoxically, the Shunamite woman is so angry that she sets out to correct the cosmic injustice that has been inflicted on her. She finds Elisha, seizes him physically and says I will not let you go until you do something. That something is not only to restore the dead child, but also to restore the sense of justice in the world.

It is precisely our inability to undo these double injustices--the cosmic one (children should not die) and the personal one (my child should not die) that make our mourning so painful. We feel we ought to be able to make our son healthy, but we cannot. We feel we should have been able to shield our daughter from that fateful car ride, but we could not. And the early days of our mourning are spent trying to come to grips, not only with the devastating death of our child, but with the almost equally devastating helplessness we feel in the face of a cruel and unjust fate.

In the story of the Shunamite woman, there are profound religious and moral issues. Elisha stands in the place of God. In some sense, we see Elisha as God. He offers life and has the power to bring back from death. But how arbitrary this all seems. Where is the justice, we want to know, in the taking of some lives and the sparing of others?

To see a child on the street who reminds us of our own, or to be with healthy friends of our child — these are acts that often produce a great deal of discomfort, and for some parents, even resentment. The basic question, "why did my child die?" remains more than a question. It remains a raw wound.

The Shunamite woman got off easily. Not only was she able to do something about her rage; she was able to restore her child to life. At least that is the apparent meaning of the story. But is that the real meaning of the story? Is there not a deeper message to be found?

Perhaps the Bible is pointing toward a different truth, one that is hard to understand, but may prove very helpful. It makes us think about the ownership of life. What does it mean to have a child? Our children are gifts — not possessions. Do we own our children? Is life something any of us can lay claim to forever? By all rational measures, the Shunamite woman should not have borne a child. But she did. She loved him very much. He was taken from her. We have to ask ourselves about the way in which that child really was present and also about the way he was taken away.

And we have to ask: was he really taken from her? Isn't it possible that that young boy is indeed brought back to life in some way so profound that makes it impossible for him ever to be taken away again? That is the comfort we seek, even in our darkest hours. The determination of the Shunamite woman is a paradigm for our own struggle to keep our children with us — to keep them forever ours.

The Shunamite woman is nameless. Her child had really died. That son, whose very possibility she had doubted, that son who came to mean everything to her was now gone. His life had been snuffed out — a stroke, a brain tumor — we will never know how he died. But he was gone, and the Shunamite woman was desperate. She went to get help. She went in anger. She would not allow this terrible injustice to prevail. She went from her house, the house of mourning, in anger, and she came back with a holy person; she came back with her faith. And then, her son came back to life. Some may say it was a miracle, and some may say it was a mirage.

But those who have lost a child know that, regardless of how we read the story, something else has happened, something transforming, something that marks the beginning of healing. The son does come back, but not in a human or worldly way. He comes back to life in a real way nonetheless. In the holy moment, the Shunamite woman realizes that her son will not leave her. The worst thing that can happen to her has already happened.

That son will remain young and handsome forever. He will live on, now in a new and eternal way. "She took up her son and they went out." How long would they be together? Forever.

The Shunamite woman, we have mentioned, is never named, nor is her husband, nor, for that matter, is the child. They are nameless, but they are symbols of life and death, and of our own happiness and despair. Each one of us who has lost could fill in the names. When a child of ours dies, we are furious. We would shake the heavens, and force the past to return as the living present. But, we are powerless. We cannot undo what has happened. No matter how often we throw ourselves at the feet of the holy, we cannot undo what fate has decreed for us.

But there are things we can do. We can create life anew. Our memories can achieve a life of their own, new life that will live eternally and through our deeds and fulfillment, new life that will bring happiness to others, and joy, even to ourselves.

Midway in the Journey

Whose pain is worse? We live in a world of comparisons. Just as we gauge ourselves by the success of others, so too, we need to compare our pain and suffering. What is worse? Is a quadruple heart bypass more significant than a triple bypass? Whose electrical outage was more devastating? Whose flood more disastrous? Who has suffered more?

We do not encourage making comparisons of the scars resulting from a loss. Every death of a child is devastating. Making comparisons is quite subjective, and doing so serves to minimize losses that are still very real and very painful. Most people might agree that losing your entire family in a fire might be "worse" than losing only one member. But, such speculations are hardly comforting. To tell someone "it could have been worse" is poor comfort indeed. As far as what is the worst loss--it is the one you are dealing with right now.

To assert that the loss of a child is uniquely devastating is not to deny the nuances and variations that are part of every unique tragedy.

The next few chapters may seem to deal with comparisons — indeed, they do. They are not quantitative comparisons; they also involve many other issues — they make an effort to understand how each different type of loss has its own unique character. It is tempting to view the differences as differences that can be measured only in terms of pain, and we are tempted to ask again, which is worse? Which is more devastating? All are devastating, but they involve a variety of factors that need to be understood and acknowledged — factors such as the age of the child, the cause of death, and peculiar circumstances involving our own individual experience. They also involve elusive issues such as closeness, estrangement and dependency. We will discuss these, and many more.

6. There Is Never Enough Time

We expect to die before our children. An orderly world demands that our children will carry on the work that we have started. It is not only the fear that we will be forgotten, but also the determination that what we have created will live beyond us. We anticipate that we will have to bury our parents—but not our children.

No matter how old our children are—no matter how old we are—the pain becomes unbearable when the order of nature is broken and the sequence is destroyed. An eighty-year-old mother is no more ready to bury her sixty-year-old son than a thirty-year-old mother can face the funeral of her five-year-old daughter. Although we are never prepared for the death of a child, there are unique emotions and unique responses that are age related. The age of our child does have an impact upon how we mourn, and it may be helpful to examine some of the unique factors related to the age of children when they are taken from us.

The loss of any child is, of course, traumatic. But there are variations in the way we mourn for a stillborn child and a mature adult child. In understanding these differences, we may find new ways to help one another and to help ourselves.

Stillbirth

Often we don't remember our earliest thoughts about becoming parents. Many of us as children ourselves, grew up in the belief that some day we would be a mother or father. As we grow older, this vague hope becomes more and more realistic. It crystallizes when we have a relationship or marriage that we expect to result in parenthood. When a pregnancy occurs, it is a time not only of anxious expectation, but also of great happiness. Month after month, we think about the baby, talk about the baby, make plans for the baby and worry about the baby. It is a wonderful time in which it is natural to have every expectation that the pregnancy will result in a happy, healthy individual.

What an unbelievable shock it is then, when a stillbirth occurs, especially if it follows an uneventful pregnancy. When our baby dies, our dreams die, too. When we arrived at the hospital, perhaps only a few hours earlier, we thought we would be coming home with a healthy new baby. Now, we are left empty and shell-shocked. If we had been expecting our first child, we are destined to go home to the house that once seemed comfortable with only the two of us — to a house that now seems strangely empty and depressing.

As authors, we have often been impressed by the spontaneity we received when people learned we were writing about the death of a child. Sitting in a beauty shop, Susan casually mentioned to her manicurist that we were writing a book that would seek to help mourning parents. Audrey said, "I can imagine it as if it was today. The doctor running down the hall, screaming at the nurse who was trying to get me to sign some forms — 'Get her in there now! I'll be responsible for her!' I had been on a monitor in the hospital for two hours. Everything had been fine until my water broke. My baby had strangled; he had suffocated. There was nothing they could have done. As long as he remained in the amniotic fluid, everything was okay. The doctor told me I was lucky — my baby would have been terribly brain damaged. I could never have stood that." Once she started talking, Audrey couldn't stop. "I could never get the image out of my mind of him strangling. I could just start crying right now thinking about it. I didn't want to see him. My husband had to because someone had to be a witness and identify the baby — but I just couldn't do it. They kept me on a medical floor, not the maternity floor. They don't want you near the babies. That night, my husband's uncle came to the hospital. He was cracking jokes; he was just trying to release the tension. I still have this image—I was walking out of the hospital wearing a teal knit dress, walking to the car, which was facing southwest—empty-handed." Audrey's baby died twenty years ago. When she is asked how many children she has, she answers, "Two living—I had three."

We have to face friends and relatives, many of whom may be sympathetic, but may say the wrong things. Who has not been told, "You're still young. You can get pregnant again," or "It was probably for the best. Something was obviously wrong with the baby." We may have to endure platitudes such as, "It was God's will. Your little angel is with God now," or, most devastating of all, "It could have been worse—it isn't as though you lost a child!" We also have to live with the fear, whether rational or not, of the question, "What if it happens again?."

Comforters mistakenly believe, sometimes crudely believe, that the stillborn child was not a real child. Still mourning the death of her child, Pam tried to explain what was troubling her. "My baby had already become a part of my life. No one can take that away from me!" Comforters who fail to recognize the power, even of the unborn, cause more pain than they could ever imagine.

Women who have had a stillborn child not only experience physical changes, but they have to endure emotional changes as well. Postpartum depression is a common phenomenon among mothers who deliver healthy infants. This depression is often the result of hormonal changes, and passes in time. But the woman whose baby dies faces a double challenge — to deal with these hormonal changes while facing the additional depression created by loss.

We have seen tremendous anger accompanying a stillbirth. This anger may be directed at the doctors, the hospital, the spouse, and even God. And sometimes it is directed internally against ourselves.

How often does a stillborn death occur without any rational explanation? How unjust and unfair does everything seem? "How could this happen? We did all the right things — we did what the doctors told us, and then some. We read every book about what to do. We ate the right foods, exercised the way we were told to, didn't smoke, didn't drink. We did nothing wrong! This shouldn't have happened to us! Look at all the parents who don't even take care of themselves and have perfectly healthy babies. It just isn't fair. Life isn't fair."

Guilt feelings are common. "What did I do wrong? Was it my fault?" We need to find some explanation for what has happened. When there is none, we may look inward. We examine everything that transpired in the preceding nine months, seeking a clue. Perhaps it was a fall or medication. "Did I lift something that was too heavy?" Sometimes there were financial problems and both incomes were needed, forcing the mother-to-be to work until the end of the pregnancy. Anything and everything can come under the scrutiny of the critical microscope.

Some parents may never see their baby, may never hold their baby. Hospitals handle the stillborn deaths differently. The practice is changing, and many hospitals now encourage the parents to spend time with their child, name their child, and hold their child.

Those who have not experienced a miscarriage or the loss of a stillborn may look upon these suggestions with horror. However, doing these very tactile things has proven to be a great source of comfort to parents who were given this opportunity. Many parents are consoled by a memorial service in which their loss is acknowledged. The purpose of such a service is to give the child an identity — there was a child, if only for a fleeting moment in time.

To be sure, there are some religious traditions that discourage mourning for an unborn child. These traditional attitudes have to be weighed against the comforting function that a memorial service can provide in a time of crisis. To acknowledge the hope of life, even in the face of death, is to provide solace at a time when consolation is so hard to find.

Young people generally do not spend a great deal of time thinking about death, either their own or someone else's. Young parents are often unprepared when tragedy strikes. For many young parents, the death of their child is the first time they have had to confront mortality. Help and compassion are needed as they enter an unfamiliar, dark time. They need wide latitude in saying and experiencing the words and feelings that come naturally at such a sad time.

How often are well-meaning people puzzled by the strong reactions of these grieving young people? They cannot understand how these parents can miss someone who had never actually been a part of their lives outside the womb. But in a very real way, the parents did get to know their child, and it is this feeling that cries out for expression. Expectant parents have spent nine months getting to know their child; they may have named the child or referred to the unborn by the name they have chosen. They have made plans—plans that are part of their own future. They may have moved to a larger home, redesigned their present house, or planned a nursery. In some cases, the expectant mother may have quit her job, intending to stay home with her new baby. Now there is the prospect of returning to work to face the many uncomfortable people who don't know what to say. What ends up being said may not be supportive or even responsive to the terrible pain.

Many of us who lose a loved one are comforted by happy memories. We recall funny times, sad times, even angry times. We can look at pictures and belongings that remind us of our child. But we who lose a child through miscarriage or stillbirth have none of those memories. Instead we grieve for a different type of loss—the loss of hope, the loss of dreams for our child. There may be other children in the future, but we will never be able to relive the joyous days of our innocence.

Infant/toddler

The instant a baby arrives home, the house is totally taken over by the newborn. Everywhere you look, in every room, there is baby paraphernalia — cribs, bright colors, pictures on the walls. Then something tragic happens. All of these bright reminders become symbols of pain. When an infant dies, there is no place we can look that doesn't remind us of the tragedy.

When an infant dies, the word "unfair" screams at us. Our baby has barely started to be aware of the huge world outside of the womb when life is snatched away. In some cases the infant may have been sick since birth. Some of these children never even leave the hospital because they are too small or too weak. In other situations, a perfectly healthy baby may go to sleep at night and never wake up. We have recently become aware of how many children become victims of Sudden Infant Death Syndrome (SIDS), that mysterious disease that we still know so little about. With SIDS, there is always the gnawing feeling that if we had only checked on the baby a minute earlier, maybe, just maybe . . .

No matter what the cause of death, parents often suffer from terrible, unforgiving recriminations, but with a loss of an infant, these guilt feelings are multiplied. "What kind of parents were we that we could not even protect or save our baby?" Even when all logic dictates otherwise, there is little comfort. No matter how many doctors, friends, and family members tell us there was nothing we could have done, we are left wondering, if only...

Most of us feel guilt in situations that could not have been prevented. How much greater is the guilt when there perhaps was some carelessness that contributed to our child's death? There are accidents that occur every day involving children. Most of us are aware of how easily they can happen. Can any of us honestly say that we have always been alert to every potential tragedy? Little children dart quickly across the street, and a second can mean the difference between life and death. Who has not turned away momentarily only to realize that returning a minute later could have spelled the difference between a nonevent and a disaster? We have to live with the knowledge that there will not be a second chance. Ultimately, we all have to live with our own harshest critics — ourselves.

We are left with constant reminders of our child. Most of us have photographs or videos of our baby, the first lock of hair, a barely begun baby book. What once could elicit great joy and laughter now become bittersweet remembrances of the child that was stolen from us.

There are social changes that occur, too. When a young child dies, social isolation often occurs. Our young son or daughter becomes identified with us and we with them. We take our child with us when we visit friends. When we go shopping or run errands, our daughter is with us. Not only friends, but also merchants and neighbors get to know her. How painful it is to return to those places alone. Some people may not have heard the terrible news and may innocently ask, "Where is our little friend today?" In explaining, we not only have to revisit our mourning, but we find ourselves in the position of having to comfort others who may be shocked and saddened by our news. And there are others who may have heard but cannot deal with the thought of something so terrible, nor do they know what to say. The truth is that no one knows what to say, yet people persist in the idea that they should be able to come up with just the "right" words.

And what if there are older children in the family? The loss of an infant sibling represents a painful dilemma for them. They, too, have needs that they themselves aren't even aware of and certainly don't know how to express. If they are old enough, they don't want to upset their parents further, so they keep their feelings inside. And if they are young, they do not know how to react, and may not even understand what has happened. We often feel the need to put up a brave front to protect our other children, but we must think of the consequences of doing so. We may create confusion for these children as well as incredible stress for ourselves.

"Without my family, I could not have gone on." Julie was in a bittersweet mood and she began to talk about the comforting role her son and daughter had played when their young sister had died. She was in mourning, but was able to feel intense affection for her surviving son and daughter. That affection was a source of immense consolation. Having other children in the house somehow challenges us with the need to at least get up and function, if only in the most perfunctory manner.

And what is the role of grandparents in all of this? An infant child likely has one or more grandparents still living. These grandparents must deal with their own pain as well as with their grieving sons or daughters. Sometimes both the parents and the grandparents try to protect each other, but only end up shutting each other out as they struggle to create a future. As mourning parents, we may expect our parents to help us, but sometimes their own grief leaves them not only unable to offer solace, but leaves us in a position where we must comfort them.

Most painful of all when we lose an infant is the need we have to confront what might have been. We have lost a vision of the future. We may never experience such simple joys that we so looked forward to—teaching our child to ride a bike, starting school, celebrating birthdays—these are things we take for granted; these are the things we hoped for. These hopes will never be realized. Parents who lose an infant are left with memories, but all too few of them.

Instead, we are also left with pain, and all too much of it.

The truth becomes so evident--no child can ever replace the one who was lost. We may have other living children, or we may have more children in the future, but the gaping hole will never be filled.

Younger Child

The death of a young child leaves us with memories. By now our child has developed a unique personality. Some of these personality traits we find delightful, others more annoying, but they are defining a human being who is precious.

"George Jr. was developing into a special, one-of-a-kind kid, and I was part of that process," George's mother, Lauren, said one day. She was finally ready to join the group and remember her fun-loving, seven-year-old son. It was his impish look that she recalled now as she talked about George Jr. As she talked about his eyes, George Sr. own eyes filled with tears.

We are fully invested in our children as they emerge from infancy and develop traits of their own. Emotional and financial sacrifices have undoubtedly been made, and we have given so much of our time. We expected that our child would be a vital part of our household for at least eighteen or so years, and of our lives, forever.

Our kids have accumulated the "stuff" that kids accumulate, and when death comes, we must now painstakingly face and sort through all of these material things that become transformed into memories. As we look at and touch each item, bittersweet memories come flooding back and difficult decisions must be made, "What will we do with this coloring book, this doll, this football?."

By now, our child is involved in school, perhaps religious education, outside interests. She has friends and we have come to know and love them. As grieving parents, we continually have to handle running into these young friends. It is difficult not to make comparisons. It can be hard to face the realization that the lives of these children will continue, apparently unaffected by our loss. Even the most giving and loving among us can wonder, "Why me?" This does not mean that we wish ill for someone else; rather, that we wonder why this happened at all, and certainly, why it happened to our child.

We may find ourselves in a virtual crisis in which we are forced to deal with our own emotions and those of our parents. Sometimes it feels as if there is nowhere to turn for strength because everyone we know is submerged in sorrow — friends, our family — they have to deal with their own sense of loss, even as they try to console us. They have their own emotions and needs, and we, in turn, are called upon to be conscious of them as we struggle to deal with our own anguish.

Lauren couldn't stop talking about her son. "They couldn't help me." Suddenly, after months of not ever being able to join her husband as he sought help, the gates were now open for Lauren. "Everyone wanted to say something, but it all came out as a blur. Afterwards I realized that they just didn't know what to say. Neither did I. Later I realized that they needed to help themselves and they just couldn't do it. No one can make sense of something as terrible as this."

When we lose a child so young, we live on with a myriad of memories. Sometimes these memories evoke intense joy—sometimes, intense pain. But, we can think of countless experiences we will never have with our child, and the pain of this realization is excruciating. Our child, for whom we wanted everything, will live only in our memories and in our love.

Adolescent

How complex it is to understand a teenager! Our teenagers bring us immense joy coupled with immense anxiety. Is a teenager an adult or a child? How much freedom is enough or too much, and when is it time to let go? Some adolescents take on the role of being a companion to one or both parents. Some adolescents and their parents are locked in constant battles and conflicts. All of these questions and all of these dilemmas become intensified and loaded with guilt and anger when our teenager dies.

Adolescence is the time where we see our child's personality develop rapidly. Our teen is able to think things through and to make decisions that will affect the rest of his life. He may have fairly definite ideas of how he wants to spend his life, both socially and professionally. He probably has formulated some hopes and dreams for his future. If we have had a close relationship with our child, we have become aware of some of these goals, and may well be in a position to encourage those goals. When our teenager dies, those hopes and dreams die too. We live with the knowledge that these dreams will forever remain unfulfilled. What a terrible waste it all seems! The worst part is realizing what we will miss experiencing together — prom, high school graduation, decisions about a career — things often taken for granted.

But not all relationships with teenagers are idyllic. Teenagers live through a period of self-assertion. They may be willful and rebellious. We recognize this rebelliousness as a vital part of growing up. What if our child is taken from us in the midst of this painful process and what if words were spoken in anger, either by parent or child — words that can never be taken back? "I told Mark he couldn't go out that evening. He hadn't finished his homework. He stormed out of the house anyway. I yelled at him, "If you go out, you'll be sorry!' Who's sorry now?" Philip started to sob, "I am!"

Philip was an insurance executive who needed to share his anger and guilt. He desperately wanted others to understand his anguish and self-recriminations over both the terrible automobile accident that killed his son and his unresolved dealings about the argument that had taken place just an hour before Mark was killed.

Once again, we see the double-edged sword of guilt and anger. Surely there are the same angers when any child dies--anger at the medical community, at God, at the world. These angers may be further complicated when our child may have contributed to his own death. We read the record of these tragedies every day — drunk driving, drug overdoses, or simple carelessness. Some parents have trouble blaming their deceased child, but we continually feel the need to distinguish in our own minds whether our children were merely the helpless victims of life's realities, or were, in some way, responsible for the tragedy that befell them. This recognition does not make the loss any easier to handle, but it does help us in dealing with the guilt and anger that so often ensues. So many of us who have trouble understanding what happened continue to need a scapegoat. We often turn our rage and blame on one another or inward — "If only you/we/I hadn't let him have the car tonight." "If only we had been more strict/more lenient." "If only..."

In dealing with our emotions, we have to recognize the tremendous impact they can have on our child's brothers and sisters. These siblings can have their own feelings of guilt as well. They may be

haunted by thoughts of, "Why him and not me?"
Fifty years after World War II, survivors, when
interviewed about the concentration camps, still
express similar guilt feelings, "Why did I live when
my parents and/or siblings were not allowed to?"
For how many men and women has that question
echoed through the years? Fifty years later, it still does.
Parents must understand that their unresolved anger
and guilt may affect their surviving children and leave
them with lasting scars.

How much more intense are these feelings when a
sibling may have been part of the tragedy himself. "It
was hard for me to even look at him. He was the older
brother; he should have known better than to have
taken his little brother skating on that pond. But then, I
realized how very much he needed me to take away
the guilt. It was hard, so hard..."

As parents, we also have to face a house full of
memories — the room, the belongings, the friends — all
the memories of a lifetime. Shall we keep them? Shall
we keep everything untouched or should we get rid of
these reminders as soon as possible? There is no rule,
of course, but we ought to allow ourselves time to
discover the path we find most comfortable.

Although one child can never replace another,
some of us decide to have more children. When a
teenager dies, however, many of us become resigned
to the fact that we are not going to have another child.
This is a particularly difficult conclusion when our loss
is that of an only child. Not only have we lost a child,

but we also are forced to deal with a complete role-change and redefinition of ourselves. Can we still call ourselves parents? Our identity, which has been inextricably tied up with being a parent, now reverts to that of a childless couple—and how painful that reversion can be.

Adolescence is a time that finds many families in turmoil. There is much conflict and tension. There may even be times when we don't particularly like our teenager, but there are never times when we don't love our teenager. And now we are left with a love punctuated with questions of what might have been.

Adult Child

The loss of an adult child carries its own unique set of problems. An adult child may have been able to fulfill some of his hopes and dreams, and may even have become quite successful. But there still is so much that will be missed.

There are, of course, many variations in the way parents interact with their adult children. If the relationship had been a positive one, they may have been best friends or frequent companions.

Ilene was nearing retirement age. She was a successful salesperson in an upscale department store. She was used to being in command of herself. The death of her twenty-nine year old son, Gil, shattered her confidence and she sought help in counseling. In one of our counseling session, Ilene was asked, "What do you miss most about Gil?" She thought quietly for a minute before tearfully answering, "Fun." Ilene had already seen her first husband die slowly and painfully, and now Gil's death was more than she could bear. It is not unusual for parents who lose an adult child to have already endured the loss of a spouse, whether through death or divorce. When this happens, the pain is compounded. The parent will have lost an important support, someone to grieve the lost child with. An already lonely task is compounded by the need to face this loss alone.

Parents may have been very dependent upon their adult child. Having children gave them some measure of security when they thought about their old age. Now, their own future has become less secure, and there is much concern about their own loneliness and care.

The very transient nature of our society may present further problems. As adults, we generally have great mobility, as well as the ability to make all kinds of lifestyle choices. Rarely do all members of a family live in the same city, let alone the same house, as they once did. Career or school may have caused our adult child to move out of town, perhaps far from us. We may have lost track of all the details of our adult child's life—his problems, his medical care, or awareness of an illness. Even when we have been aware and involved, there was only so much we could have done to help, because as adults, our children make their own decisions. The very distance that separates us can make our pain more profound and more distressing.

Surely, aged parents are not immune to feelings of guilt, as they watch an adult child suffer and die. Many parents realize that they cannot control the situation. But that does not alleviate the guilt they feel. After the death of their child, they realize that there was more they could have done to influence the child in terms of crucial medical decisions. "When my son lived at home before he got married, I made sure he ate the right things and saw his doctor regularly, and took care of himself." Some wish their adult child had switched doctors or tried another method of treatment.

Jan was in a bitter mood. Not only was she angry at her husband — he refused to come with her to the group, but she was also reviewing once again the poor medical treatment her daughter had received while she was suffering from Crohn's Disease. "I knew the doctors weren't doing the right thing. I wanted her to try a different doctor — a different hospital. She kept saying she would, but that her HMO would only pay for the treatment she was getting. She said that maybe they could save the money to go somewhere on their own. I was so frustrated — I felt helpless. She kept saying she would handle it." Of course, these are only "what ifs", but they haunt the parents, and add to their already considerable guilt and anger.

And if our adult child lived out of town, it is probable that we did not see her as much as we would have liked. How we wish that we had called or visited more often.

The death of our child may be a sudden one, or there may have been warnings that death was near. Some of us have been able to be with our child during the final phase of an illness. It is torture for parents to get on a plane to attend their child's funeral, and it is especially difficult for us when our child is buried out of town. Whether we are cemetery-goers or not, many of us find comfort in knowing that our child is buried close to us--that we could go to visit the cemetery, even if we don't do so regularly. When a burial takes place far away, this option is taken from us.

Jan was becoming more and more upset. She began to cry softly. "Karen was buried where her husband and children live. Then I just found out that they are moving to another city. I can't stop thinking of Karen being alone. I hope that someday we will be able to move her to a cemetery close to us. I just don't want her so far away all by herself."

And what about the very elderly? Amazingly enough, very elderly parents of mature children can even be overlooked entirely because so much emphasis is placed on the younger members of the family. Helen's story may be an aberration, but it is a warning. Helen was 92 years old when her son, a very successful doctor, died suddenly of an aneurysm. The family gathered to tell the clergyman about the deceased. During the service, the clergyman recited the names of the wife, the children and very close friends. But something was troubling. He noticed an elderly woman sobbing quietly in the front row of the mourners. Who was she? The family forgot to tell the clergyman that Samuel's mother was still alive. Helen's pain, so intense, was multiplied by her family's failure to acknowledge her.

And what about our grandchildren? We have such tremendous concern over their well-being and future. We are concerned for our son-in-law or daughter-in-law--can he/she manage alone? Is there enough money? Who will take care of the children? As grandparents, the bittersweet memories are indelible reminders of our child as we look in the face of a grandchild and see our own child's reflection.

But what if there are no grandchildren? Surely it is sad to realize that we will never have the enjoyment of watching our child parent our grandchildren. Not only does this make us aware of the grandchildren we will miss, but, makes us even more cognizant of our own mortality and the probable demise of our family line.

And after all we have gone through what more could happen? The spouse of our deceased child begins to date. We may often find it very difficult to understand that our son-in-law or daughter-in-law could do such a thing. Logically, we know that this will happen, but it can also be problematic. We like to think that our child's husband or wife feels as strongly about our child as we do. When her son-in-law, whom she had always adored, started seriously dating a woman within months of Karen's death, Jan was furious, "How could he do this to her? Didn't he care about her at all? I feel like I don't even want to talk to him. And, how can he do this to our granddaughters?"

We will almost invariably be disappointed and hurt if we expect a son-in-law or daughter-in-law to feel and react just as we would like. Everyone mourns differently, and the reaction of parents is unique. If the dating process starts too "soon" we may become angry. We may resent that a spouse could "replace" our child. We wonder how she could "forget" or "get over" our son so quickly. Some parents do admit that they could never accept another relationship, no matter how long their son-in-law or daughter-in-law waited. Difficult as it may be, we need to face the fact that life goes on for other people, even though ours seems to be at a virtual standstill since the death of our child.

Finally, there are the words that hurt us — "He had a good life." Friends say that with the best of intentions, but the words are searing. To the parent, even of an adult child, that is just not enough. No matter how old an adult child, a parent never stops being a parent.

7. Into That Dark Night...
How Did Your Child Die?

W
e are never ready. The final moments still come as an incredible shock.

In our experiences, working with bereaved parents, we have learned not to compare losses to determine which is the most devastating. Of all the tragedies we endure, the loss of a child falls into a unique category. As parents, though, we often cannot resist making comparisons, "No pain can compare to mine."

As counselors, we are quite aware that society seems to have set up a hierarchy of losses. A subtle message tells people where their loss fits on an imaginary continuum. Even in their intense grief, some parents upon hearing of another tragedy can be heard to ask, "That would be worse, wouldn't it?" Or, "Isn't that the worst thing you've ever heard?"

Questions such as these are always uncomfortable for those of us who seek to console, for they reveal a deeper need that many parents have — a need that is expressed in a faint hope: the hope that in the company of sorrow, they might find some consolation. To agree, "Yes, that would be terrible — much worse than what you are going through," would surely diminish the importance of their loss. Does the realization that things could be worse really mitigate the pain? There is no answer to such questions. If we agree, we risk the danger of stifling genuine feelings and suggesting to parents: "Since things could be so much worse, you shouldn't be complaining and feeling sorry for yourself."

The reality is that grieving parents still have the ability to feel pain and sadness for other grieving parents. When they hear someone else's tragedy, parents have often been heard to say, "What a nightmare. I could never have handled that. That would be just too hard."

What type of loss is the worst? It seems folly to debate this question, but we have come to recognize that losses are different, and that each has individual components that make it unique. Each situation is special, just as each child is special. Recognizing the universal components in the death of a child, we nevertheless have determined that by analyzing the causes of a particular death, we can help comfort parents in more specific ways.

When Death Follows a Long Illness

"At least you weren't surprised." That is what parents sense they are hearing after their child has died following a long illness. This is simply not true; when death occurs, there is always a degree of surprise. Of course there is not the shock that accompanies a sudden death, but, until death actually occurs, it is never known precisely when life will end.

"I knew it was going to happen, but I didn't expect it to happen then," we hear from numbed parents. Even after a long, difficult vigil by a child's bedside, these are not unusual words, "I just didn't think it would be so soon. I just wasn't ready."

There is always hope. Until the very end, there is always hope. No matter how optimistic and unrealistic, this hope is precisely what allows parents to survive the nightmare of their child's prolonged illness. They cannot allow themselves to give up at a time when they need all the courage and strength possible to be there emotionally for their child. It is impossible, and possibly not even advisable, to be totally emotionally ready.

A long illness is exhausting for the family, both emotionally and physically. By the time the parents are through taking care of their sick child for the day, there is neither time nor energy left to devote to other children whose needs do not stop because there is a sick sibling. Other children feel neglected, left out, or less important. Brothers and sisters may feel resentment or anger toward both their sick sibling and their parents.

Taking care of a sick child at home is a full-time job. Life at home bears no resemblance to what it was before. The home suddenly is filled with all sorts of apparatus, people may be temporarily relocated to a new place to sleep, schedules will invariably change, and life as it once was will be put on hold for an unspecified period of time. The house that was once filled with joy and laughter becomes an ominous place that is scary and uncomfortable; people have to whisper and alter their normal behavior to avoid disturbing the sick child.

Even after death, the house will never seem the same again. It is hard to banish the images of sickness. How many homes are sold within a few years of a child's death? Just before Lisa died, Nancy and Steven had a beautiful home with a swimming pool. Now they had sold it to move to a condominium development. Nancy and Steven seemed an unlikely couple. She was a schoolteacher who was very quiet and into her own thoughts, and Steven appeared to be a gregarious salesperson who found it difficult to take no for an answer. "After Lisa's suicide, our house was wrapped in a cloud of silence. It was too quiet. We just walked around like zombies, barely speaking to each other. We knew that something had to change. We needed to be around people." The house had become a memorial—a very sad one.

The suffering of someone we love produces within us an agonizing sense of helplessness. Although we live in a time when there are constant advances in pain control, pain is so often a component of illness, especially in the later stages. "The worst thing was seeing Jeremy in pain and knowing that I was totally helpless. There was nothing I could do." To realize that they have no control over what is happening can cause parents to experience extreme anger, sometimes to the point of rage. The memory of the pain is something that stays with us even as we cannot fathom why our child had to suffer. That our children had to die is incomprehensible enough to all of us, but the pain of watching them suffer makes our sadness even more unbearable.

A long illness is often accompanied at the outset by a time when our child is still feeling strong and healthy. This "picture of health" makes it all but impossible for us to accept the reality of the diagnosis. "How can they say my daughter is so sick when she looks perfectly healthy?"

In retrospect, many parents treasure the memory of these comparatively happy days. They talk about how each "good" day was a gift to appreciate. For some families, this was a time to do something their child had always wanted to do: take the family to Disney World, get the puppy he had been wanting, just spend more quality time together. Even the simplest experiences become very precious, and families can become much stronger and closer.

This is a time for good conversation, too —
thoughtful conversations. The topics can become
serious, even touching upon death, religious beliefs
and fears. Many parents try to avoid these
conversations. They may want to shelter their child by
not sharing the facts with him. We believe this is a
great mistake. Children know that something is
wrong — even the youngest of them. Parents are often
blind to their child's awareness. Children not only
want to talk about what is happening, but need to talk
about it. It is terribly sad when a dying child feels the
need to protect his parents, and therefore can confide
in no one.

We hear so many stories about children who had
to resort to waiting for a doctor or nurse to arrive in
order to have any real communication about the issues
on their minds. Too many children have waited for a
quiet night in the hospital to confide in an
understanding nurse, "Can you keep a secret? I am
gong to die, but my parents don't know. Please don't
tell them because they will be really upset."

When parents are afraid to broach the subject of
death, fearing that their child will not be able to handle
it, this often means that the parents are having more
difficulty discussing death than their child. Children
are worried and want to be reassured that everything
will be all right. For them, death does not have to be a
frightening abyss. Young children do not inherently
fear death, but know that it must be something terrible
if their parents won't discuss it.

Likewise, a family needs to be able to cry together once they openly acknowledge their impending loss. Parents who have a fear of crying in front of their children may fear being seen as weak or out of control.

As upsetting as it may be for children to see us cry, there are moments when our crying may even comfort them. It is at intimate times such as these that children see us as human, that we have feelings as they do. They can see how much we care, how deeply we feel. Surely, we don't want to turn our child's last days into an ocean of tears, but we need to acknowledge that there are moments, and our child will almost tell us when they are, when our crying becomes a healthy, crucial outlet for the flood tide of emotions.

When there is a long illness, families may have time to spend together, to laugh, to cry, to hug and kiss. "I love you" can be said with genuine authenticity. There is an opportunity to say good-bye. People whose children die suddenly sometimes spend months, even years, agonizing over the fact that, "We didn't even get to say good-bye." Those of us who have watched over a dying child need not reproach ourselves on this score. Prolonged illnesses allow us these opportunities.

No book written in our generation would be complete without a mention of AIDS. So many parents have lost children to this horrible disease. Parents watch their children suffer for years with this debilitating illness. AIDS eventually causes even the most mature victim to become a dependent child again. Parents may end up taking care of their adult child as they did when he or she was an infant. They watch helplessly as their child becomes totally helpless, as they see the wasting process take place.

Unfortunately, there is still a stigma attached to AIDS, which makes it even more painful for families to handle. Parents face so many decisions: Shall we discuss it? When shall we discuss it? With whom? There may well be members in the immediate family who refuse to acknowledge AIDS, who are judgmental toward the ill child, and who even blame the parents.

In the case of a gay or lesbian child, there are other issues. Parents may not have been aware of their child's homosexuality or may not have wanted to acknowledge it until confronted with the diagnosis. Not only do they have to accept their child's fatal illness, but they have to deal with their own feelings about his or her sexuality at the same time. There may be incredible stress within the family, even between the two parents, who may have different views about homosexuality or how to respond to it. These parents may not be able to support each other because of their divergent views. At a time when parents need to talk about what is happening, shame and embarrassment may stifle their communication. They may well become isolated from one another. In other types of illnesses, friends and relatives rally around, but families affected with AIDS may find themselves abandoned.

At a time like this, friends may seem judgmental; some are literally terrified. They may want to help, but are just too afraid to do so. This fear does not have to be logical. We know so much about AIDS intellectually, but no amount of knowledge can allay deep-seated preconceptions and prejudices.

Although emotional issues are paramount, there are also practical consequences. Financial problems can be overwhelming when there is a long illness. Even with insurance, there are many expenses that are not covered. These place an undue burden even on families that are fairly comfortable. They can be devastating to a family that was already struggling before the illness began. In cases where there is no health insurance, what starts out as a problem quickly turns into a financial nightmare. Financial obligations incurred during a prolonged illness can affect the life of the family long after the child's death.

A long illness, no matter what the cause, alters the rules of life for all the members of the family. Everything changes, as the emphasis shifts from jobs, friends, play, and life as it was before, to caring for the child. Once death occurs, the family is faced with the enormous task of rebuilding their lives with few tools and with only the vaguest idea of where to begin. After a long illness, we can hardly remember a time before our days were consumed as a nurse or companion to our sick child. When that final moment occurs, we may feel confusion and emptiness about who we now are, and what our role will be. It is as if a job has been completed, and we are no longer needed. The emptiness can be devastating.

When Death is Sudden

All sudden deaths have one thing in common—the survivors are shocked and unprepared. Our lives change permanently—literally in a second. Survivors cannot even comprehend what has happened, "I just can't believe it! It is impossible!"

How often do we call someone to tell them some bad news, and the response is "You're kidding!." Of course the person knows that we would not be sadistic enough to joke about such a serious matter. Yet, disbelief is an understandable reaction. The mind needs time to adjust to the shock, and denial is a way of hoping that the tragedy isn't real. How can there not be shock when something so devastating is totally unexpected? "I just spoke with her yesterday," or "I just saw him last week, and he looked fine!" Is there any one among us who has not been shocked to hear the news of the death of someone who was, or was thought to be, healthy?

The word "shock" takes on new meaning when applied to the death of a child. "How could this happen? Children are not supposed to die!" Our minds like things to be predictable and orderly—the death of a child is neither of these. Our thoughts are full of disbelieving questions: "Why him?" "Why now?" "How did it happen?" And the inevitable,

"What if...?" And the devastating guilt feelings: "Why did I let him...?" "Why didn't I stop her?"

Is there ultimate comfort in the knowledge that our child did not have to suffer? Such small consolation is overwhelmed by a sense of shock and anguish. There is no opportunity for anticipatory grieving, as in the case of a long illness. In cases of sudden death, all of the grieving begins in one moment, and the intensity grows and grows and grows.

There are so many unanswered questions and some will never be answered. Brian and Ilene regarded themselves as loving and responsible parents. Then their adult son, Gil, died suddenly of acute pancreatitis—and their lives were shattered. More devastating was the knowledge they acquired from their son's friends. Gil had taken antacids for years on a regular basis. He had never seen a doctor for his problem. Bill and Ilene couldn't believe what they were hearing. Had Gil been aware of the gravity of his condition? How could he have ignored it for so long? These parents had to deal with feelings of anger at their son for ignoring a situation that could have been controlled by diet, medication, and exercise. They also had to deal with their guilt for not having been aware of his health problems. For Brian and Ilene, the inability to get answers was the source of ongoing frustration. Nothing could have changed the outcome, but they felt they needed to know certain things, and it was the suddenness with which the tragedy unfolded

that left them confused and angry. Could anything
have been done? What if the ambulance had gotten
there sooner? Why didn't Gil know that he had a
problem? Or did he know? Questions such as these
haunt parents for weeks, months, years—a lifetime.
Feelings of futility are part of a sudden death. It all
just seems so unfair—so random. The death of a child
taps into our innermost insecurities: Life is so fragile;
we can't count on anything.

Devastating in a unique, incomprehensible way is
the violent death of a child. An accident or murder
elicits many of the same thoughts as any other death.
But another dimension has been added. Something or
someone was responsible. Here, too, the knowledge
that the death could have been prevented is
excruciating. Many violent deaths may be attributed to
simply being at the wrong place at the wrong time.
There was an accident, a drive-by shooting. We never
expect the victim to be "my" child.

When our child dies suddenly, the tragedy is
compounded by the fact that there is no chance to say
good-bye, or to tell her how much we love her. More
likely than not, we were not there when our child met
her death. We are left ridden with guilt. Not only were
we unable to protect her from this terrible fate, but
more critically, we were not there at the right moment.
It does not matter that there was nothing we could
have done to prevent the tragedy. Emotions take
precedence over logic, and the feelings of guilt are
overwhelming.

And what if there were misunderstandings? It is bad enough when parents say good-bye to their child and never see him alive again. It is another thing entirely, if, during their last time together, they shared with angry words. Our grief becomes even more intense as we replay that last conversation in our minds. Like a scratched record, the scene repeats itself over and over again.

And what if the parents bore a share of responsibility for the death? Perhaps the most devastating feelings of guilt occur when the parents played a role in what happened to their child. Tom was an intense manufacturer's representative. He was also a workaholic and an alcoholic. He had been drinking and ran a red light. His car collided with a railroad abutment. Although he was unhurt, his daughter was killed instantly. For years Tom relived the scene. "How could I have done it? How could I have let it happen?" Only after months and months of talking with other guilt-laden parents was Tom able to reconcile himself to the disaster that so tragically altered his life.

Guilt is not merely a passive shadow hanging over our lives — it may become so overwhelming that it can lead to substance abuse, suicide, divorce, or other problems. Perhaps this is why so many parents feel the need to rationalize what happened — to lift the blame — to reorganize their lives so they are not continually reliving the same awful scenario.

In times of tragedy, parents feel so helpless and powerless. They experience such a total lack of control over what happened to their child that they look for something to lift their child's death out of the tragedy itself. They need to feel that "my child did not die in vain." The need on the part of these parents to continue their child's life by finding some sort of meaning has led not only to countless contributions to families and communities, but also to the creation of various groups, such as Mothers Against Drunk Driving (MADD), Parents of Murdered Children, etc.

The suicide of a child is most parents' worst nightmare. Suicide leaves its indelible scars on a grieving family. If other deaths may have been avoidable, then suicide is the most avoidable of them all. It is so difficult to accept and understand. We live in a society that does not view suicide as an acceptable solution to a problem. Our religious traditions universally frown on suicide, and many religions have specific sanctions against it. At a time of suicide, parental grief is multiplied. Anger, guilt, and shame are intensified. After a suicide, there are so many questions that the survivors would like to have answered, and they often cannot shake these doubts and questions.

Suicide still carries a special stigma. Unfortunately it also carries a fatal attraction. Those who know a person who committed suicide often wonder whether there was something they could have done to prevent this final act. "I just saw him last week. If only I had taken him more seriously." If we, who knew the person only slightly, feel guilty, we can only imagine the intense feelings faced by parents.

And how quick some foolish people are to blame parents. "Why couldn't they have been more aware?" "Why couldn't they have prevented the tragedy?" "Didn't they even know their own child?" If you have ever seen a parent tell others that his child took his own life, it is impossible not to recognize the pain, no matter how many years have passed. One only needs to meet a couple socially and ask an innocent question, "How many children do you have?" The anguished look of these parents is unforgettable.

A suicide in a family creates a whole pattern of insecurity. Once parents have a child who takes his life, they never feel totally secure about their other children. They may become overprotective, controlling, or mistrusting. The contemplation of a second suicide is too much to imagine.

Even years after her daughter Lisa's suicide, Nancy was still unable to accept the consequences and changes that had occurred. She remembered how she and Steve could no longer endure their beautiful new home and had decided to move to a modest condominium. Now there was the looming possibility of a divorce. To make matters worse, Nancy was having uncomfortable feelings about another daughter. Lisa's younger sister was showing signs of depression. At a counseling session, Nancy burst into tears, "I can't go through that again. I would not be able to survive."

Evan was an only child who took his life. We have come to know his parents well. Month after month they come to find consolation. They find it only in the compassion they receive from other mourning parents who recognize that as deep as their own loss is, the suicide of an only child is a tragedy beyond all tragedies. For so long, parenting was a major part of life. Now nothing. No hope. No future. Are they still parents?

The loss of any child, at any age, through any circumstances, is so very devastating. Whether death comes as a relief from endless pain, or as a complete shock, our lives as parents are forever changed. Can we find ways to change that are meaningful and life-giving? That is our task — our challenge.

8. Bonds that Can Never Be Shattered

Every parent-child relationship is uniquely different. Just as we do not have identical relationships even with identical twins, so too, there is something so unique in the special way we relate to our child. We can never duplicate what we have experienced. To say that no one can ever replace our child is certainly a truism. But we soon come to realize as we mourn that more than a death has occurred — a whole way of relating to another human being we loved and often adored has been terminated forever.

We may have other children, we may find other people in our lives whom we love, but the particular way that we felt about our son or daughter will always remain unique. No one can understand this the way we do. There was a bond that only the two of us shared, and now that bond has been transformed by death. No one can ever precisely understand the pain of our loss. They may be able to empathize or even sympathize, but they cannot totally comprehend exactly how we feel or what we have experienced.

Can we expect a mother and father to react in identical ways to the loss of their child? In many cases they do, but it is more than likely that parents have their own separate bond with the child they have lost. In Chapter Twelve we will look at how these differences affect family relationships, but for now it is important to understand the folly of expecting any two people to react in the same way to a tragedy. Mother and father are unique. They both love their child, but their love may take different forms and bear different histories, as will their grief. Mother and father may remember different things. They want to cherish their own memories.

When our child dies, part of us dies too. At the same time we have to understand that there are differences that are created by history – the record of each parent and child is different. In some cases there was extreme closeness and nurturing. In others, estrangement may have occurred. Ambivalence may have marked the relationship of still other parents and children. As painful as it is to recognize, there are cases in which a parent-child relationship was not an ideal one.

While we certainly acknowledge that intense pain over our loss is present whether the parent-child relationship was close or distant, it may be helpful to look at the various ways parents and children interact with one another. The point is not to draw value-loaded comparisons, but to suggest that an understanding of the peculiarities of relationships can guide us as we seek a path toward healing.

Close Relationships

Your child shares your home. You are in constant contact. Children who are young are part of almost every activity and decision that you make. As your son or daughter becomes an independent adult, you maintain regular contact, either by phone or in person. This is what happens when the family is close and the feelings are warm and loving.

We are used to being able to pick up a phone and speak to our adult son or daughter. What a wonderful feeling we have when we can enjoy such closeness with our children. "My son was my best friend." Malcolm was recalling all of the good times he had had with Lawrence before his adult child had been shot down by a vengeance-filled former employee. Malcolm and his wife, Priscilla, always sat sedately and seemed somewhat aloof from others in the group. Malcolm repeatedly talked about Lawrence as if he were not only his son, but his insurance policy for his old age, someone who would maintain the corporation that had been his family's mainstay for fifty years. "We worked together every day. But it wasn't only about business. Whenever we could both get away, we would meet at the country club for a round of golf. He was always my first choice of partners." As he said the words, Malcolm turned to Priscilla. He needed her to understand his special emptiness. Priscilla, ever under control, reached out her hand and gently placed it on top of Malcolm's.

The loss of that warm relationship produces feelings so intense that they are actually frightening. Life has lost its meaning. There will be no more private jokes, lunches, phone calls, shared thoughts and feelings. That we will never see our beloved child again is too much to comprehend. We are aware of an actual searing pain—a physical as well as an emotional pain.

We who were close to our children are blessed with happy memories of good times and good conversations. Although we worry that we will forget some of these memories, we are a part of them and they can never be taken away from us.

Is there such a thing as a perfect relationship? Probably not. And we have to admit that there are times when nostalgic feelings suppress those less than ideal memories. This is a natural consequence of a generally good relationship. We don't want to remember unpleasant times when everything else was so beautiful—nor do we have to. Indeed, in an ideal family it is often true that the very moments that we might consider difficult were those that drew us closer together.

No matter how much time we spent with our child, most of us feel that it was never enough. No matter how many experiences we shared, we feel cheated — deprived of the opportunity to have more of everything — especially time. When we have been fortunate to have really enjoyed one another, the time spent together will forever remain too short. As parents, we invariably wish we had spent more time, paid more attention, avoided working so hard at tasks that took us away from our families. We yearn for anything that would have given us more precious time with our child and more memories to sustain us through our loss.

Surely, when the family was close, the death of a child may lead to unexpected bitterness. The idyllic relationship has ended and cannot be replaced. The very nature of the relationship was uniquely ideal, the loss of that relationship may multiply our anger. We become aware that the ideal can never be duplicated — with other children, with husband or wife, with friends. Frozen in time, the love of parent and child becomes something that seems almost holy.

But, when we are close to our son or daughter, we can also find great strength in beautiful memories. We can be easier on ourselves. We can realize that, although the book of life is never complete, we were able to experience an incredibly beautiful love during the years spent together. There are bittersweet memories, of course, but with time the bitter may be reduced and the sweet enlarged.

Distant Relationships

But what if the relationship was not idyllic? When we
envision parenthood, the dream of closeness seems
quite attainable. Adults do not deliberately choose to
become parents so that they can live out dreams of
endless frustration and disappointment. Some parent-
child relationships are deeply problematic. Why is
this? The reasons are many and varied. We don't know
why two people can meet and find an instant bond
between them and others can meet and experience
only distrust and enmity. But we do know that not all
mothers and fathers can find in their children the
perfect relationship that our society seems to expect.

Does this mean that we made a mistake in
becoming parents? Does it mean that we did
something wrong? That we were not strict enough?
That we were too demanding in our expectations? Or
perhaps we were not adequately qualified to become
parents in the first place. How manifold are the
opportunities for self-recrimination and guilt, even
under the best of circumstances. How much more so
when our relationship with our child was a troubled
one.

As they grow, children are lured by all kinds of
behavior that can harm them—gangs, drugs,
premature love affairs. Most troubling to many of us is
that our children are not always willing to listen to our
advice. Even when we try to forbid behavior we know
to be harmful, we can be met by anger and
rebelliousness. Our efforts to do what we know to be

best can be frustrated by a child who simply will not listen. And we are often left disappointed and angry.

How frequently have we heard a friend of ours jokingly ask, "Do you want him?" The question, so often asked in good humor, may contain a serious undertone. But just try to take that parent up on that offer! Most of us recognize that frustrations, disappointments, and difficulties are part and parcel of raising children and watching them grow into individual human beings. But we are seldom overwhelmed by these thoughts. More often than not, we are forgiving and secure in the knowledge that everything will work out in the end. Alas, there are times when relationships simply remain sour and neither love nor understanding can bridge the gap between the ideal and the reality.

And what if our child dies while the relationship is still a distant one? What confused feelings we experience! Yes, the years of heartache and strife are over, but so is everything—including the potential for any kind of reconciliation and closeness. That potential will never be achieved. We are left with feelings of anger, guilt, disappointment, and sadness over what might have been and now can never be.

Some people think that when a parent-child relationship isn't strong, parents will feel less anguish during a loss. The opposite is often true. Unresolved issues commonly intensify pain. When such a death occurs, we must once and for all accept that we will never have the closeness we had been yearning for. We have lost not only the years when our child was alive, but also the potential for a loving and warm relationship. Through all those years we had hoped that someday things would turn around — that they would get better with the passage of time. Now, we are left with our memories. Perhaps things were not quite as bad as we thought they were. Some of us try to rewrite the history, and doing so helps us to ease the pain. And perhaps, in reality, the reconstruction can actually become a pact of peace between parent and child.

Ambivalent Relationships

In reality, most parent-child relationships are neither perfect nor hostile. If we were truly honest, many of us would have to admit that the relationship with our child contained elements of ambivalence, "I love you, but..." More than one parent has said that to their child. Certainly, many of us have not liked all the things our child did. We learn the hard way that our child and we are not interchangeable, and therefore, he does not act or feel as we do in all situations. Friction resulting from our child's behavior can create some very ambivalent feelings, "I love you, but..."

When we are in an ambivalent relationship with our child, death may cause our pain to be more complex and difficult to understand. We review our child's life and find so many things that could have been done differently. If only our son or daughter had really understood. Some of the disagreements may now seem petty and insignificant. Why were these things so important then? Why were we so stubborn? There are no meaningful answers. We find it hard to justify the problems that occurred or the positions we took.

We want to feel that our relationship was perfect, but we know that it was not. We are left with the nagging feeling that we were so close, but something went wrong. What if we had only listened more carefully? What if we could have spent more time together? What if we had been a little more open-minded?

The "almost" in our relationship also produces a sense of frustration of a different kind. We feel that so much has been wasted — our time, our emotions, our child's precious days. Was it so important to be right — to have our way? Did it really matter how long he wore his hair, or how short she wore her skirts? Things that once seemed worth arguing about become irrelevant. But then we thought we had all the time in the world.

We all recognize that over time our priorities change and things do not have the same importance or value they once did. We have to realize that death brings a rearrangement of the most basic values. It is natural for us to want to rework our memories. We wonder whether there was more we could have done. Why didn't we try harder? Why didn't he try harder? Guilt permeates our thoughts. It is at times like this when we need to understand that each relationship is unique—that we did the best we could and that our guilt serves no useful purpose. We can allow ourselves the healing balm of memory. Whatever regrets we have are best served not by bitterness, but by a new dedication to those around us. How to achieve this dedication remains one of the crucial tasks that we must yet confront.

9. Anger

I've really never been an angry person; now I find myself feeling angry about everything!

"It's not nice to get angry."
"Stay calm."
"Control yourself."
"Stop it!"
"You're out of control."
"We'll talk about it when you calm down."
"He can be nice, but you have to watch out for his temper."
"She seems angry all the time."
"Come on, don't be mad."

These are some of the messages that we have been given about anger. Anger at a time of great loss assumes a life of its own. It may be helpful to take a look at what role anger plays at such a time and how it has so often been suppressed.

You may recall warnings about anger from your childhood. However it was expressed, the message was clear: It isn't "nice" to show your emotions. Mature people are in control. For many, these tapes from childhood are imbedded deeply within us.

When we hear something often enough we start to believe it. By the time we are adults we have been socialized to the point that we don't even have to fight these feelings anymore. They are so deeply buried that we are no longer even aware of their existence. On the rare occasion when we find ourselves feeling angry, we chastise ourselves ("Aren't we being ridiculous?") and often deny our feelings. We tell ourselves to calm down, as we question the intensity of our feelings ("Is it really that important?")

When we lose a child, everything becomes so incredibly painful. As parents, along with our deep sorrow, we must also confront our anger. In other words, we are forced to handle emotions that may have been successfully buried since childhood. Now, not only are we devastated, but we have to deal with an anger that makes us feel childish or immature.

When we lose a child, what are we angry about? It would be easier to ask what aren't we angry about. The simplest, most mundane things can infuriate us — the weather, our friends' behavior, our own behavior. We can even be angry with our child, or our God.

When we lose a child, we are not only bereaved, we are totally disoriented. And we are forced to change our lives in such dramatic ways that our anger often becomes the only bridge we have between a past that has been destroyed and a future that is terribly uncertain.

Ilene was more than frightened. The loss of her first husband followed some years later by the devastating death of her son, Gil, had driven her to the point where every memory brought tears of anguish. Her second husband, Brian, was as supportive as any husband could be. Although Brian was not Gil's biological father, in reality he had been everything that a father could possibly be, having helped raise Ilene's three children since they were small. And now, they together needed professional help. Ilene sat tearfully, touching a strand of her hair. She kept talking about the acute pancreatitis that had caused Gil's sudden death nine months before. The passage of the months did not find Ilene comforted. Rather, each day she found herself feeling worse. She cried frequently, and was unable to function in any comfortable fashion. As she told her story, it became clear that for years her son had ignored his body, masking his symptoms with huge quantities of antacids. Gil had actually contributed to his own avoidable death. Although Ilene's son hadn't caused his condition, his lack of responsibility and refusal to take care of himself drastically shortened his life. "Aren't you angry," Ilene was asked. Ilene could not accept the truth. All she could do was cry and say, "That would be so terrible. How can you be angry at someone who is dead?"

Only gradually did Ilene come to the realization that was so uncomfortable for her — that she really was angry — angry at the hospital, angry at the doctors, but most painfully of all, angry at her beloved son. Although Gil had the right to deal with his life as he chose, his mother had every right to be angry with him. Gil's negligence had caused so much pain for others in that it deprived them of their relationship with him. Just because you are angry with someone doesn't mean that you don't love them. That was the reality that Ilene gradually came to accept.

We all have had to face relationships in which we loved someone, but couldn't like or accept everything the person did. What a relief it was for Ilene to be able to face the fact that she could still love her son, but could also give voice to her anger. She felt as if a cloud had been lifted. "You gave me back my life," she sobbed one day. "You told me it was okay to be angry." For Ilene and for others, getting in touch with anger is a valuable tool in building a new life.

There are so many potential targets for our anger. The easiest one to focus on, and the most non-threatening, because it is impersonal, is the medical community. We can spend weeks or months agonizing over whether anything could have been done that would have caused a different outcome. We can be angry with the 911 operator, the paramedics, the ambulance driver, the hospital, the doctors and nurses, and even at the researchers who had not found a cure in time to save our child.

We have to admit that sometimes this kind of anger can serve a utilitarian purpose. It allows us to focus on something and to bring a sense of the rational back into our lives. Someone had to be at fault. This anger can even provide a break from the intense emotional sadness that has enveloped us.

There can be anger about the funeral — who came, who didn't come, what they said, how they acted, even what they wore. Once the anger begins, there is often plenty of it to come out. We may even be angry at the clergyperson for one of many reasons — she didn't say enough, he said too much; he talked about himself the whole time. The funeral home is another target of anger. A sensitive funeral director, just like a sensitive clergyperson, comes to anticipate this potential reaction.

Sometimes our anger is directed toward strangers. Tom and Beth could not stand to go to a mall or restaurant where there might be children. The mall seemed to be a focal point for all of Tom's guilt. Every time he would see children there he would remember that terrible night when he had drunkenly driven his car into a railroad abutment, and he remembered Mary, that innocent five-year old whose life was suddenly snatched away. Both Tom and Beth felt more than uncomfortable with any couple who had a family — they were resentful. For some of us, their resentment may have seemed irrational, yet it occurs too frequently to ignore. A baby shower or birthday party, joyous events for the whole world, become occasions to dread, occasions to avoid. "My child should be here. Why can't my daughter have a birthday party — ever?"

Just the knowledge that something happy may be happening to a friend's child can be so fraught with anxiety that by the time the day arrives, we look for excuses in order not to attend. We actually feel isolated, and in turn, our own behavior can distance us from people who do not fully understand what is going on in our lives.

Our spouse may well become the most obvious and accessible outlet for our anger. As husbands and wives, we may be angry with each other for many reasons. For one thing, we may handle grieving differently. These differences tell us that our spouse doesn't feel as we do, doesn't understand us, didn't really care about our child in the same way we did. Our interest in sexual activity may be hampered by our anger. One spouse is often ready to resume sexual activity before the other is prepared to do so. In moments of anger, it is not at all unusual for one spouse to feel that the other spouse bears some responsibility for the terrible tragedy that has befallen the family. At the very least, he or she should have done more to prevent it.

Anger may also be present in our efforts to return to a so-called normal social life. What if one parent is ready to socialize before the other is? Nancy and Steve were prominent political activists in their suburban village. They had a host of friends and entertained frequently. They played golf at their country club and Nancy loved her weekly bridge game. Then their daughter took her own life. After a few months Steven wanted to go back to the country club to play golf, to resume the Saturday night dinners they had so enjoyed. But Nancy was far from ready. "I had to pretend — to put on a happy face for the world. I was just not there, and Steve did not understand."

The differing rhythms in which parents mourn need to be understood. One parent may feel coerced into staying home in interminable sadness. He would rather go out and try to find some brief pleasure from being with others. The different tempos may result in resentment and loneliness. "She wanted me to just sit in the house with her. How long can we just sit in the house and stare at each other? It was like a tomb. So depressing. It's not that I didn't have pain, or that I am over it — I just have to get out — to be with some people."

In Chapter Fourteen we will deal with the role that our faith in God plays in dealing with the loss of a child. But now we have to understand that God is not immune to our anger. This anger at God is hard to deal with because it is so often accompanied by tremendous feelings of guilt. Religious people are troubled by their feelings toward God at a time of such tragic loss, but also by their anger at what God has done to them. How could He do this to me, to my child, to our lives?

We are confused — what kind of a loving God would do such a horrible thing? We have seen angry parents turn away from their religion, feeling that it no longer has meaning for them. The very foundation of their beliefs has been shattered. The collapse of a traditional trust in an all-loving and merciful God can be very devastating to people who have relied on their faith. It can be doubly devastating at a time when faith is desperately needed. Can we return to find comfort in our religion? Many parents can, and do. That return is often filled with mystery and self-discovery.

Even our friends can be objects of our anger. How often do we feel that our friends do not understand what we are gong through? People often say or do thoughtless things. How fortunate we are when our friends remain constant and when they are able to respond to our changing moods and needs. Even friends who were involved at the time of our loss and shortly after, sometimes seem to disappear; leaving us alone, feeling abandoned.

It even happens that within a few years of a child's death some parents find themselves cultivating a whole new circle of friends. They may still see some of their old friends occasionally, but more for reasons of tradition than closeness. We hear it said often that "old friends are the best friends," but many of us are drawn to new friends after a tragic loss. We feel more comfortable with people who have gone through similar experiences. We may feel we can talk more freely with someone who really understands what we have gone through. Have they not traveled the same long road?

Parents may lash out in anger toward other family members, other children. Things large or small may disturb us in profound ways. Sometimes we are even angry that one child survived while another did not. How tragic it is when one of our children becomes the scapegoat, a victim of emotions that we cannot understand or control. "Your brother would never have done this. Why did the smart one have to die?" "Your sister was on her way to becoming a doctor, and you just waste every day at the bowling alley. What's wrong with you?" Our disappointment and anger are heaped upon the hapless survivors of a family tragedy. These feelings can seldom be fully understood, seldom justified.

The most difficult anger to acknowledge, let alone deal with, is the anger we have toward our deceased child. We try as hard as we can to deny its existence, but, when it is there, it is especially painful. How can we be angry with someone who is dead, who cannot defend himself? But anger is an emotion. It does not have to be rational.

Sometimes this anger is obvious. When a child contributed to, or caused, his own death we may find it hard to separate our anger from our grief. So, too, when there is substance abuse, reckless driving, or suicide. Even when there is no blame to be placed on the child, we may still feel that the very death is a betrayal. Our child has deserted us; through his death he has deprived us of the relationship that was so precious. We need to learn to acknowledge our anger. We need to accept it. And, eventually, we need to be able to forgive. That is often a formidable task, but a necessary one, just the same. Our anger is real and it needs to be acknowledged. It can take many forms and it can attack many victims. Getting in touch with these feelings may be difficult and threatening. But acknowledging them is an important step toward wholeness.

10. Guilt

We have seen how easy it is to feel anger at a time of great personal loss. Much more complicated, but equally prevalent, is the sense of guilt that so often accompanies our anger. How often these two emotions — guilt and anger are tied together! We feel guilty about feeling angry, and then, angry with ourselves for feeling guilty. We may even recognize that there is little or no justification for our guilt feelings, but these feelings are present nevertheless.

Why does this happen so often? We all look for explanations and often for someone to blame. Blame is a way of understanding and making things logical. If we can assign blame, we can feel better able to understand what has happened to us. There is always a need to find something that we could have done or something we neglected to do that could have changed what happened in our lives. When we are realistic, we recognize how pointless much of our blame placing is. If something could have been done, surely we would have done it. But so often, we remain convinced that there is something that we must have missed. What tremendous recriminations we heap upon ourselves for something over which we had absolutely no control. These feelings of guilt can persist for months, even years. They defy logic. Nothing seems to dissipate these debilitating feelings.

Not only do we feel guilt about the circumstances surrounding the death of our child, we feel guilty about how we are mourning. We can be so hard on ourselves that at a time when we need to be kind and gentle to ourselves, we set up idealized and unrealistic standards about how we should be behaving, how we should be grieving.

"Shoulds" play a powerful role in the grieving process. Besides feeling that we should have been able to save our child from death, there are so many things we think we should not do--not cry as much, not talk about our child, not compare our child with others. To our own detriment we create a straitjacket around our mourning—one that ties up our need to express our emotions openly and honestly. The constraints make us feel that we should be perfect, under the most imperfect circumstances imaginable. By placing these unrealistic demands on ourselves, we set ourselves up for failure and for the perpetuation of the guilt cycle. When we cannot live up to these imaginary standards, we add guilt to the already long list of emotions we have to deal with.

The guilt we feel is associated with how we see ourselves as parents. We feel that we should have been able to protect and shelter our children from any possible harm that might come to them. And we have failed. When a child dies, we have to deal with these feelings of failure. We have not been good parents. We failed our child in their most important moment.

As parents, we are so often plagued with feelings of worthlessness and low self-esteem. A frequent lament is this, "What kind of parent am I if I can't even save my own child?" These feelings of shame, embarrassment and guilt can sometimes seem overwhelming. The feeling that we have failed as parents can be devastating.

But we are not omnipotent. We ought to realize how much power we try to assign to ourselves when we assume that we have so much control over life and death. Of course, at a tragic time in our lives, power is the last thing we feel we possess. Something terrible has happened to us and we can't handle it. We can neither understand it nor control it. The power that we attribute to ourselves is the power we think we should have had, the control we should have exercised, the outcome we feel we could have changed. We should have the power – and we find that we don't.

Our guilt always assumes that we could have changed the outcome. It fails to recognize that there simply are situations and events that are out of our control. By surrendering some of this power, we may discover that we have surrendered some of our guilt and that we can be more comfortable with ourselves. But what if parents justifiably have some reason to believe that they caused, or, at least, did not prevent their child's death when they could have done so? Even when these deaths resulted from an accident, some parents choose to never forgive themselves, and are doomed to carry this knowledge with them. They imagine themselves stigmatized, ostracized or pitied. The result may be years of self-hatred.

Only months after the accident that had killed his daughter could Tom admit how drunk he had been at the company Christmas party. He remembered how he had gone to pick up his daughter at dancing class. He remembered how the teacher had smelled his breath and begged him not to drive. "I'm all right," he said and grabbed his daughter's hand and led her to the car. He even remembered speeding through a red light and the moment the car was crushed by an oncoming van. Tom could never get over the experience of remembering how his daughter was pronounced dead at a nearby hospital.

For years Tom had to live with the guilt that never seemed to leave him. In addition to that burden, he felt stigmatized and ostracized by those who knew the story. And, indeed, he was ostracized. How can those who still care about Tom, despite his terrible tragedy, try to help him?

There is nothing harder than dealing with the double pain of loss and guilt. In some way, all of us know that what happened to Tom could have happened to us. How many of us may have driven when we had had too much to drink, or when we were impaired in some critical way? Or perhaps when there was a blizzard that should have told us to stay home?

Guilt feelings may be impossible to overcome, but the realization that none of us is perfect and that each of us is a precious child of God should both lead us to ease the stern judgment we impose upon ourselves and to treat others with equal compassion. An "accident" is not an "on purpose situation." We cannot control every aspect of life, and bad things, of course, happen even to good people.

Our minds always struggle with the diametrically opposing forces of logic and emotion. Although logic is reasonable and rational, emotions, especially at a time of crisis, can be overwhelming. It doesn't seem to matter what we know; what matters is how we feel. People constantly try to reason with us, trying to point out our faulty thinking. You can tell us hundreds of times over many months that we did what we could, that there was nothing more that we could have done. You can ask us what more we could have done, and we will not be able to think of a thing. To any effort at rationalizing our guilt, our response will always be something like, "But, maybe..." or, "If only..."

That, at least, is our response until we can grow to be truly realistic, to recognize the distinction between the fantasy and the reality, between what happened and what might have happened. To do so is to recognize the power of our emotions. Emotions may be embarrassing or uncomfortable to talk about. We feel that people think we are foolish for the raw feelings we often have. And indeed, people sometimes do feel that way. They may be frustrated over their own inability to convince us that we did what we could have done. They may exhibit impatience when we seem stuck in our guilt. Surely we know that we did what we could have done, but how hard it is to avoid feeling that we could have done more. "If only I had been a better parent."

To deal with our guilt, it is often helpful, and sometimes imperative, to have as much information as possible. For example, we may wish to make an appointment with our child's physician. To have a doctor assure us that everything that could have been done was done may not console us, but it relieves us of some of the responsibility we may have heaped upon ourselves. Relieving guilt is a matter of time and talking it through, over and over and over. Blessed is that time when we become tired of placing guilt upon ourselves, when we know it doesn't belong there. There is a time that comes when we can acknowledge in our hearts that we did what we could, and we can finally rest assured of it. That knowledge is much more comforting than a constant litany of guilt.

Anger and guilt are very much a part of mourning. They are feelings that we are not always proud of. They can be difficult to get in touch with. People who have not lost a child often ask, "Why are you angry? What do you have to feel so guilty about?" The question itself is devaluing to our feelings of self-esteem—feelings that are already at a low point. These questions serve to deny us our genuine feelings and doubts—feelings that we have to work through in our own time. We need to recognize the genuineness of our emotions. Friends and acquaintances who deny us our opportunity to do this are simply adding another level to our guilt. Not only are we feeling guilty, we are feeling guilty about feeling guilty! When we cannot accept our feelings of guilt, we simply deepen and lengthen our grieving. Grief hurts, but not grieving is even more painful.

As we have seen, it is important to understand the close relationship between anger and guilt. These feelings are genuine and need to be accepted both by parents and by those who seek to help them. It is all too easy to judge these feelings and to seek to control them. What is important to accept is that they are real and that by understanding them we can move beyond denial to healing.

11. Changed Hopes
-Changed Lives

Time does not bring relief; you all have lied
Who told me time would ease me of my pain!
I miss him in the weeping of the rain;
I want him at the shrinking of the tide.

Edna St.Vincent Millay
(from "Renascence Sonnets, II")

Is it really true, as Edna St. Vincent Millay suggests, that "time does not bring relief"? The question itself contains a parable and a promise. Time heals—time heals nothing. The realization that both are true is itself a form of relief. How does the paradox work?

Several years ago, a young social worker asked if she could come to one of the meetings of our group,

Parents Who Have Lost A Child. It was important for her training, she suggested. She would not say a word, she promised. She would merely observe and learn. And so, she came and sat.

The parents gathered in silence. New members of the group are invariably silent. They do not know what to expect, or what is expected of them. They sat with the young social worker and waited. And then, the meeting began.

Parents sitting in a semicircle began to tell their stories. One mother told of visiting her son in a Houston hospital. He was a prominent doctor and she watched him slowly die of leukemia. Another mother described in tones chillingly devoid of emotion, how her own husband had purchased a gun, taken their daughter out into a field and fired a bullet through her head. Then he turned the gun on himself. Older members of the group had heard these stories before, but even the group's veterans found it hard to listen to some of the details. Everyone could understand the anguish of the mother who had watched her son slip away, but they were unable to fathom how a parent could kill his own child.

How could a father kill his own daughter? And why were these parents, already experiencing their own grief, willing to subject themselves month after month to a recitation that was so bizarre and incredulous? Yet, these parents did not want to stop their monthly meetings with one another. How can you tell someone to stop coming to the one haven where they can vent their innermost thoughts? The stories of parents who have lost a child turn into sagas — too powerful for any fictionalization.

The evening wore on and story followed story. The young social worker sat and listened. And then she began to cry. "I know how you all feel," she blurted out. "I just lost my grandmother a few months ago." That session ended with thirty enraged parents vowing never to let an "outsider" into their meetings again. To lose a child is unlike any other loss. To lose a child defies comparisons.

In truth, the death of a child is different from any other loss for a wide variety of reasons. It is different not only because of the intensity of pain it evokes, but also because of the duration of the mourning period. "Why aren't you over it by now?" parents are asked. But they are not over it, and in a way, they never get over it. More than one parent has said, "We don't get over it — we just get on with it."

Part of the paradox we spoke of before is that the very process of *seeking* comfort makes us aware of how distant comfort is. The more parents try to "get over it", the more mired in their grief they become. Society regards mourning as a "healthy" response to a loss, or a deep sadness. But is it wise to think of mourning in terms of "health"? Actually, mourning is neither healthy nor unhealthy. It is a reality. And it is the most unreal thing we will ever know. In the loss of a child, the reality of unreality is something that persists for a very long time. There, we said it: "for a long time." In truth, for some parents it persists forever.

You don't "get over" the loss of a child. You don't begin to "feel better." You don't even experience a "healthy" mourning period. All of these terms fail to understand the changed status of heartbroken parents. The simple truth is that those of us who have lost a child become changed people. It is not only that something precious has left us; it is that something has entered — an unwelcome and shadowy presence — a presence which will not allow us to return to our old ways.

Phrases such as "feeling better", "healthy mourning period", "return to normalcy", while often used to describe the stages associated with other bereavements, fail to recognize the changed status of ourselves as parents. It is in vain for us to seek to return to the person we were before. Our focus is not on a return to an Eden that can never be re-entered. Our focus, rather, should be on the creation of a new life — a new life that recognizes the tragedy of separation, but allows us to move on.

One night we decided to bring reminders of our children to one of our parents' sessions. Some of the parents heard that this might be helpful and others talked about how difficult it was to deal with the material objects of a past that can never be resurrected. And so, despite some reservations, our group determined to share with one another the physical objects that were precious to them.

It was a strange collection of memories that our group had assembled on that cold February evening. Beth came with a doll that had belonged to her daughter. "This is the first time I have been able to hold it," she explained. "This is the first time I have been able to go back to her room." "I can identify with that," Ann said. "I could only bring this photograph. I could never even walk past Trudy's room—that's why we finally just had to sell our house."

The landscapes of our lives change. A bedroom can become a shrine for some parents. For others, it can become a taboo place as well, a place that becomes desecrated merely by entering it. Parents may want to take down the room or preserve it, stay in their home or move from it as quickly as possible. Old vacation spots may be visited with new reverence, or avoided as places of unbearable memory. The exteriors of our lives become transformed as *we* become transformed by our loss.

What we discover as we come together after a tragedy, is that we all respond in recognizably different ways. Yet we all feel that we are no longer the same person. Death itself has caused the transformation. It has carried us over a threshold into which we know we have been forever changed. No amount of preparation could have readied us for what we now feel ourselves experiencing.

As parents who have lost a child, we may, in turn, have friends whose own child is critically ill. These parents sometimes turn to us in the hope that we might offer them magical words that will ease the pain they fear they are about to experience. In the face of a hopeless diagnosis, these parents seem to be imploring: "Prepare me for what I may have to face." But no preparation is ever possible. Oh, it is possible for parents of a desperately ill child to realize that the inevitable moment is destined to occur. But no amount of planning really prepares us for the decisive change that occurs when the end actually arrives, nor is any other separation really analogous to the actual death of a child.

A mother phoned us to say that she and her son had become estranged. He had moved to California. He would have nothing to do with her, nor she with him. "May I join your group," she begged, "and mourn my son?" Our group discussed her request. The parents were unanimous. "Tell her to go and find him," the parents pleaded, "tell her to hug him and tell him she loves him." Estrangement is a bitter separation. But it is not death.

Not only do we respond differently to our losses in emotional ways, we may also respond in ways that affect our physical well-being. The loss of a child can exact a physical toll. It is not unusual for the death of a loved one to be followed by the onset of a serious illness. Physicians have noted that mourning parents seem to be accident-prone. The evidence may be anecdotal, but it occurs often enough to warrant our attention.

More often, parents who have lost a child complain about their ability to concentrate. In the middle of a conversation, they might start to resurrect the past. For a brief moment they might fantasize that they are about to meet their son for lunch, or that they are going to greet their daughter as she steps off the bus. Their minds will fleetingly wander back to experiences that will never come again, to moments that can never be repeated. As depressing as the sadness, these grief-stricken parents can never explain to those around them why they are so distracted and why they are feeling so disoriented.

How often are sleep patterns affected by the death of a child? "I have lost so much sleep," William confessed, "I don't feel effective at work anymore. I don't feel right taking home a paycheck." William's college-age daughter had been killed in an auto accident, and William was the one who had to identify her body. The vision of that tragedy had come to haunt him, and to rob him of his sleep. Yet, as he described his wakeful nights of terror, another mother in our group smiled. "What is so amusing?" he asked. "I do nothing but sleep," she replied. "Sleep is the thing I do best. I could become a sleep therapist. It is waking up that terrifies me."

Often our eating patterns change, too. One of our mothers lost her daughter due to complications resulting from bulimia. Perhaps it should not have been surprising when that mother complained that she had been unable to eat since her daughter's death. But then other parents came forward to suggest that they, too, were experiencing changed eating patterns following the death of their children. "I can't eat." "I can't stop eating." The list of physical changes that may invade our lives seems endless.

As varied as are the somatic reactions to loss, the psychological changes that occur are even deeper and more subtle. Again, the variety of responses is less significant than the awareness of the fact that real changes are occurring.

It is helpful for us to recognize all of these external and even internal changes as they occur. It is important to realize that our sleep patterns, our eating patterns, and even our ability to be patient with others may undergo dramatic transformations. Understand, too, that these changes are not unusual and they need not cause panic. But it is also important to recognize changes that may lead us in new directions. Armed with our new insights, we may actually grow in marvelous ways. We may actually become more patient and understanding. We may find, even to our surprise, new compassion and deepened trust.

Do these changes occur immediately? Surely they will not become apparent in the first tragic days or weeks following a loss. Like a young sapling, they may take years to reach their most fruitful expression. It is important to understand not only the changes that the shock of loss creates, but also the changes those years of absence and yearning produce.

Aren't we entitled to feel that after all we have suffered, we can ignore some of the limitations society places on our behavior, and live as we wish? Our society generally regards altruism as more to be desired than selfishness, but mourning parents may feel they are justified in ignoring the judgment of society. They may feel it perfectly appropriate to live in a way that fulfills their own desires. "After all, I have suffered; am I not entitled to some happiness?" The truth is, though, that ultimately we actually find immense satisfaction and relief, too, in reaching outward. The ability to reach out to the world, to forget our own interests, at least periodically, in favor of helping others, is one of those things that many of us may initially find so hard to do, yet ultimately find so satisfying.

Priscilla was a lady of great dignity. It was obvious that she understood what it meant to travel in the most comfortable of circles. She could not reconcile herself to the death of her son, who had been murdered in an act of vengeance — shot by an angry former employee. "I no longer care about other people. I do not want to hear about their problems. I've got my own, and, that's more than I can handle." But Priscilla's husband, Malcolm, reacted in quite a different way. "Since Lawrence's murder, I've become even more compassionate," he said. "I know what it is to suffer, and now I know how to reach out to others who are suffering." Priscilla and her husband found it difficult to reconcile their two widely different views of life following the death of Lawrence.

For years, Priscilla remained stoically within the emotional shelter she had built for herself. But then things began to change. Was it the influence of her husband? Was it the passage of time? One Sunday evening she volunteered to serve in a local soup kitchen. "I'm beginning to accept other people," she announced one evening. "I'm doing it for Lawrence."

It is time to return to the paradox; time heals — time heals nothing. How do we get over our pain and return to emotional health? If we think of health as something that can be quantified or prescribed, the answer is never. Whether Priscilla rejects the people around her, or opens up her heart to the wounded and oppressed, she does so with the persistent consciousness of her beloved son. That consciousness is forever part of the landscape of her life.

Our memories may break into consciousness with less frequency as the years pass — that is the healing that time brings — but they remain eternally on the cusp of our consciousness. And, those who mourn would have it no other way. A return to "normalcy" is impossible because the loss of a child is so unlike any other loss. No, we do not want to forget. To forget is to deny the memory of our son or daughter. To forget is to diminish our love. To forget is to betray something basic in human nature--the need to preserve our past even while we create our future.

"I came back tonight," said one father to our group, after an absence of many years. "I came back because today is the twentieth anniversary of my son's death." "And what has happened during the years?" one member of the group asked. "I've changed. I've made peace with myself. It gets better, but it never goes away. I wouldn't want it to go away. I need to keep his memory alive. If I forget him, it would be as if he never lived. And, by God, he sure did live."

12. The Family In Transition

We are living in a time when the security and stability once associated with childhood can no longer be taken for granted. Increasing dissatisfaction with the political process and its leaders, a growing disparity between the very wealthy and the very poor, combined with an indifference to voting give evidence of this insecurity. When we see so much violence on our television sets and learn, for instance, that in one year hate sites on the Internet have doubled, we can understand why increasing numbers of people find themselves disconnected and dissatisfied. On a personal level, except for a very few of us, more and more people have to confront the fact that there is little if any job security. And many of us face growing concerns about Social Security, Medicare, and our entire future.

"Family values" is a slogan that evokes a past that was tranquil and predictable. When we think of stability, we think of family. More than anything else, the word *family* conjures up images of security, comfort, constancy and reliability. Home is the place where we can really be ourselves, relax, let our guard down, and allow our vulnerabilities and emotions to show. Things may not be idyllic in a family situation, but the elements of family lead us to think of such commonplace things as dinners, schedules, personalities, and a host of factors that are generally predictable.

And then a child dies.

When that happens, everything is disrupted. Everything is different. The entire family changes. The family, as it was, is gone. A new family may evolve—a family with an entirely new structure. That new family will include the surviving members and will incorporate the memory of the deceased child. The process will take time and will not occur without substantial pain.

In this process, tension is inevitable. Family members need to develop new relationships among themselves and to learn to deal with one another in new ways. For example, our children may hesitate to talk about their sibling for fear that it may upset us. In turn, we as parents may feel uncomfortable talking to each other in front of our children. So often we feel that we must show a brave front to the children. We do not want to appear weak or out of control. A redefinition of power and bravery is often part of our new role as grieving parents.

But these new relationships are not without problems. Surely it would be more helpful if we would allow ourselves to talk freely in front of our children, or if we could encourage our children not to stifle their thoughts. Whenever there is a perceived need to act in a way that is dominated by concern for others, stress is inevitable. Too often, it is at those stressful moments when closeness and communication are so important, that a breakdown of communications occurs. Instead of helping one another, barriers are created that are difficult to tear down.

Can we truly shield other family members from our sadness? Countless parents admit the only time they allow themselves to really cry is when they are alone in a bathroom, a bedroom, or in their car. For so many parents, this car is not only seen as a place of aloneness but it becomes a symbol for escape. "I couldn't wait to find any excuse to drive. I would create fictitious errands, just to have that escape valve. I would feel relieved when I got in my car alone. I felt that I could have feelings without hurting anyone else."

Brian, who never hesitated to express his feelings, was typical of many parents who seek escape in movement. He said, "As a television repairman I was on the road all day making house calls. It was the strangest thing. The minute I got into my car between calls, I would cry and cry, thinking of Gil. Then when I got to my next client, I would go in, have my appointment, do just fine. Then I would get back into my car, and the same thing would happen all over again. I had to keep my feelings bottled up so much of the time, that when I could let them out, I did. It felt good — like some stress was relieved and I could go on." What Brian could express alone in his car he could not express with other human beings. It was more than two years since Brian's son had passed away. He and Ilene found themselves unable to reach one another emotionally. "Whenever Ilene and I are watching television and something sad comes on, I get up and leave the room."

Ilene couldn't understand Brian's behavior. "I thought that was your way of avoiding the issue and telling me that you didn't want to talk about it." In reality, Brian had not wanted Ilene to see his sadness. He desperately wanted to talk about their son, but not at the cost of further upsetting his wife.

The inability of Brian and Ilene to express themselves to each other kept them from helping each other at a critical time. As two people who had usually been able to support one another in ways that no one else could, they now found the door closed. Unfortunately, these two caring people, without ever realizing what they were doing, were denying themselves the unique support shared only by those who knew their child most intimately and who loved him most deeply.

In trying to bridge the communication gap, a mother and father may turn to a self-help group or counseling, or sometimes they come alone to a counselor in search of help. It is not unusual for one parent to feel that he is just fine, it is she who needs help. "I'm okay, but she is having a hard time."

These differing perceptions tend to place one of the parents in the role of the "healthy survivor" and the other in the role of the "disabled one." The "healthy survivor" does not need anyone else – does not need to talk to anyone or be helped by anyone. The "disabled one", on the other hand, becomes the "weak" spouse – the one who needs attention and support.

The images of weak and disabled are very misleading. Even recognizing that parents are very different from each other and mourn in widely different ways, we make a big mistake if we associate the need for help with weakness, and a retreat into silence as a sign of strength. To be aware of our feelings and to recognize our need for others may actually be strength. To be stoically silent may be a symbol of weakness – not invariably, of course, but often enough that we have to recognize the possibility that silence may actually be a deafening cry for help.

To recognize this truth is not to deny what we have often confronted – that different people react differently in the same situation. Parents have their own individual ways of grieving. One may want to discuss the loss constantly; the other may want to grieve silently. One parent may want to discuss the loss when out with friends; the other may want to focus on other things in order to find respite from the constant pain. One parent may want to become involved in social activities in order to feel alive and escape from the sadness for a few hours; the other may not feel like socializing, putting on a happy face for the world.

Some parents are reluctant to enjoy themselves when their child is no longer present to share with them. Movies had always played a prominent role in the relationship between Alice and her grown daughter, Marsha. The two had gone to the movies together every Saturday afternoon for as long as Alice could remember. Marsha had bought a new video recorder just preceding her death. And then she died suddenly, in her sleep. After the tragic loss of her daughter, Alice took the video recorder to her home, thinking that watching movies might now be comforting to her and her husband. Several years later, she told our group that the video recorder was still in its original box—unopened. "I won't even let Frank set it up. He keeps saying we could be watching movies. He just doesn't understand. How can I watch movies? I should not be able to watch movies if Marsha can't watch them."

It may sound inconsequential, but even a simple VCR can be the focal point for tension and misunderstanding. Even something as mechanical as dealing with that recorder can demand patience, understanding, and compromise. Often these are the very qualities that are so hard to find at a time of distress, a time when nothing seems understandable, and when anger and bitterness make compromise difficult.

Should it surprise us to discover that sexual stereotypes, too, may influence grieving patterns? In our time, these stereotypes have begun to evaporate, but images of what a man "should" be like still prevail. A man should be strong, and should be able to support his wife through her emotional traumas. Our society still seems to believe that it is more difficult for a woman to lose a child than for a man. Don't women more easily express their emotions in public than men do? In our experience, fathers suffer every bit as much as mothers when their child is taken from them. All too often, they are expected to do so in silence. It is not "macho" for a man to show that he is having difficulty handling a painful issue. Men are expected to somehow work through their problems and then be available to help their wives. It is an expectation that is terribly unfair.

Many of us still believe that women grieve more visibly and for a lengthier period. This expectation often produces an inequity in the way men and women are treated in the workplace. When a woman returns to work, her coworkers tend to be more supportive. They may make allowances for under-performance. She is handled with kid gloves, and people say, whether in words or actions, "Be nice to her — she lost a child."

Fathers, on the other hand, may be greeted with a different response when they return to work. The sympathetic words are there, but are soon replaced by an expectation that everything should quickly return to normal. Men are expected to jump right back into old patterns. They are allowed a brief grieving period. Many coworkers expect that period to be completed by the time they return to work.

Often the words expressed to the grieving father are simply, "How is your wife doing?" Philip echoed this common reaction with a mixture of anger and anguish. "At home, I was so concerned about my wife and her feelings that I couldn't even think about how I felt. When I returned to work, I thought it would be different. I thought I would be able to be myself. But no one asked me how I was doing. Did they think that I could handle it? I pretended, because they expected it, but no, I couldn't handle it." Once again, misleading stereotypes are reinforced. The message is, "Be strong."

Strangely enough, work can be a great comforter. Many working parents can't imagine what it would be like without their jobs to return to. Work is what saved them from retreating into a shell. "If not for my job, I would never get up in the morning, never see anyone or talk to anyone." What a tempting thought during intolerable grief. Work, whether paid or volunteer, facilitates our grieving process by giving us something outside of ourselves to focus on. It is important to feel that life is not just passing us by, but rather that we are still, at least in some small way, a part of life—a meaningful work life.

Returning to work too soon, however, may create its own problems. Even a good thing can be overdone, and work is no exception. Problems occur when work is used as an escape from home or family, or when someone becomes consumed by work in order to avoid grief. When we stifle our feelings by work or other artificial means, we often find these repressed feelings emerging later in more complicated ways.

As an accomplished certified public accountant, Andrew was responsible for a large staff of accountants. Paradoxically, Andrew's son died during the tax season—the busiest time. Andrew's bitterness was mixed with a deep sense of guilt. "I have no choice. Too many people are depending on me. I can't let my clients down. I'll think about it after April 15th." April 15 came and went twice, and this man had still never allowed himself to grieve for his son. Only when he became aware of the fact that his being "too busy" may have severe repercussions in the future, did he allow himself to mourn.

Work is one of the great integrating forces in our lives. In addition to providing us a livelihood, it offers purpose and meaning. It allows us to be creative and productive. Work, too, is often an arena where we can regain control of our lives. At least during the hours we are working, we can feel in control, able to act and make decisions. At a time in our lives when so much has been taken from us, we can find one area where we need not be helpless and dependent.

What of nonworking parents? Often, these parents have said that they had to force themselves to have something planned for each day or they would have stayed in bed. "There didn't seem to be much point in even making the bed or getting dressed. Nothing had any meaning, and the normal activities were too trivial to even bother with. One day just turned into another, and I neither knew nor cared what day it was. I just wanted to hide, to make everything go away."

In so many instances, having something to do, anything at all, helps. Sometimes we are reluctant to do things that might bring us a little relief to our sadness. Steven and Nancy found that to be a tension in their life. "A year after our child's suicide," Nancy said, "I didn't even want to go to Thanksgiving dinner with the family. I couldn't imagine what there was to be thankful for. Steven wanted to go, so I went reluctantly, and was glad I did. Staying at home wouldn't have helped. In fact, I would have just gotten deeper into my isolation."

How often anticipation is worse than the actual event. Nancy's reluctance about Thanksgiving evidences a phenomenon that occurs frequently. The anticipation of the dreaded event takes on a life of its own.

We count on each other, husbands and wives do, to cheer each other up when we are down. This works well when sadness affects one of us more than the other as when one of us loses a job or a parent. It does not work as well when both parents are living through the same personal torture. On the surface, it seems that it would be easier for two people going through the same torment to support each other. In reality, it does not always work that way.

No two people grieve in the same way. This is something we have said so often, yet it bears repeating. Instead of feeling supported, one or both partners feels abandoned by the other. These discrepancies may manifest themselves in communication, readiness to socialize, or even in the area of sex. The simple realization that one may heal more slowly, or recover more quickly, can have an estranging effect. We have so often noticed how profoundly the sex lives of grieving parents become problematic. One parent may feel an urgent need to resume normal sexual relations in order to feel that a comfortable pattern of life has been restored while the other may find sexual overtures cold and uncaring. Some may not even want to be touched or held.

Steven felt safe to bring up a subject that had troubled him for many months. "I needed to be close to Nancy more than ever. I saw her hurting, but I was hurting too. I thought we could comfort each other." Steven's thoughts wandered off as he remembered that terrible moment when he and Nancy returned home, smelled the gasoline fumes in the garage, and found Lisa slumped over the steering wheel.

But Nancy was not willing to let the subject drop. "How could he even think that way at this time? Sex was the last thing on my mind. I felt physically dead. I was constantly exhausted and I felt like I could barely get up in the morning. I knew I was disappointing him, but I just couldn't feel a thing."

Anger can play a large role in the decreasing desire for sex. In the deepest sense, isn't that what created the problem in the first place? If we had not created a child, we would not have lost a child.

Not only anger, but also feelings of embarrassment may accompany the sexual act. Parents may feel that having sex is to act in a way that is disrespectful to their deceased child. Since she can no longer do anything that might be pleasurable; why should we? Does resuming sexual relations mean that we are over our grief? Of course, sex is more than a physical union between two people. It involves deep-seated feelings and emotions that we do not always understand. These feelings may cause tremendous friction between parents, often driving a wedge between them at a time when distance is the last thing that is helpful.

When parents are spending so much energy simply trying to survive, relationships with their other children may suffer. It's easy for a sibling to feel rejected when so much attention is being focused on their brother or sister who has been plucked from the midst of their family. Did my parents love him more? Why couldn't I have been the one to die? These are typical of the thoughts that invade the mind of a surviving brother or sister for months, even years.

Johnny was seven at the time his older brother, Charlie, died. Johnny couldn't understand all the sadness that was swirling around him. He tried to put it into words; "My parents don't seem to care about me. All they talk about is Charlie. They look so sad all the time. I wonder how they really feel about me. My dad used to take us fishing with him. A few days ago, I tried to get him to take me, but he wouldn't. I guess he really only cared about going with Charlie all along."

If we adults do not understand death, how much more difficult is it for a child? Irrational thoughts and fears abound for adults and children alike, but especially for children. They are flooded with frightening thoughts. Was it my fault? Will it happen to me? Will my mother leave me too? My father? How often are our children surrounded by guilt or shame — they have survived and their brother or sister has not.

Although parents may be guilty of ignoring their surviving children, more frequently, they become overprotective. The fear of another loss is so strong they want to control everything the child does in order to assure his safety. This leads to a double resentment. The overprotected child feels that his freedom has been taken away, and in turn, resents the brother or sister who "caused" this to happen. Of course, this resentment leads to more guilt, more self-recrimination.

Is it surprising that a surviving brother or sister will try to please the parent by trying to take the place of the one the parents loved so deeply? These survivors want their parents' sadness to stop. One way is to symbolically become the deceased child so that the parents will not miss him so much. Mark had always worn a baseball cap. His brother, T.J., never did. But in the days after Mark died, T.J. went to the closet and took out Mark's old baseball cap and started to wear it. Not only was T.J. grieving the brother that he missed so much, but he was also telling his parents that he could take his brother's place. In this family, T.J.'s parents could recognize what T.J. was doing, but so often this attempt to imitate leads to disappointment and frustration. No child can ever take another's place. What a sad experience it is when the efforts to do so intensify the pain of loss rather than diminish it.

Children grieve in unique ways. The loss of a sibling may create fears that last a lifetime. Before their brother or sister died, our child's only experiences with death might have been hearing about the death of someone else's grandparent. In some cases, they might have experienced a death of a goldfish, or seen a dead animal by the side of a road. They are certainly not prepared for the confusing feelings that surface when faced with the death of someone so close to them--someone they thought would be with them forever. And adult siblings may face an even more difficult task. The responsibility of "carrying on the family name" may lead to an intensification of pressures. The death of a sibling can also increase anxiety about one's own mortality.

Even in their short lives, our children have learned that old people are supposed to die before young people. So what happens when a brother or sister dies? They immediately realize that something is not right. Children like things to be predictable and orderly. They are used to routines and knowing what to expect. Suddenly everything is topsy-turvy. Nothing makes sense. Our children may be dealing with their own fears. Do children die? Does that mean I could die too?

Teenagers have a particularly difficult time with death. They view themselves as adults and should be able to handle everything, including the abstract idea of death. But teenagers are very vulnerable to the death of someone close to them. The scars often last for years. When a classmate dies, these young people are typically overwhelmed by grief, and the confusion that occurs as a result of a tragedy is undeniably profound.

When a death occurs in the family, teenagers may react in a totally different way. In addition to the sadness, which they inevitably experience, they may feel that they have to be strong. They are aware of younger children who look up to them. They are aware of the vulnerability of their parents and want to help. But where can they turn to find help for themselves? These teenagers are in the vulnerable position of having nowhere to go to vent their feelings.

A sensitive teacher or counselor is invaluable at this time. Even under normal conditions, the teen years are filled with considerable stress and confusion. When a teen-ager loses a brother or sister, this confusion is heightened and the feeling can become terrifying. They can feel a sense of vulnerability about their own bodies and their own lives. When a brother or sister dies, their sense of invincibility becomes challenged. Nothing will ever be the same again.

In truth, the entire extended family is affected by the loss of a child. Grandparents who must face their own grief have to deal with an added burden. In addition to their own sadness, they have to endure seeing their own child hurting so much. They feel a sense of frustration. They know that they are unable to help their child through the incredible pain that cannot be avoided. How grandparents handle such a tragedy depends upon historically entrenched relationships. If there were not open communication and discussion in the past, it would be unrealistic to think that the bereaved parent would choose to turn to the grandparents for comfort now. For their part, grandparents will feel a double loss, particularly when they see their children looking to others for support. While mourning for their grandchild, they also mourn the relationship with their own child.

Brothers and sisters of mourning parents often represent a different kind of problem. As supportive as they may be, they are sometimes cast into negative roles. "My sister never cared about Gil when he was alive." Ilene was reliving the disappointment she felt at her time of greatest sadness. This evening her bitterness was directed against her own sister. "She always pitted her children against mine and made everything into a competition. Now she says I won't talk to her about Gil. She complains that she doesn't know how to get through to me. She's right—I won't talk to her. It's a little late now."

How often we turn to friends rather than family for comfort. As natural as these instincts are, they often complicate the stresses which inhibit the relationship between the nuclear, and extended, family.

But isn't there a more positive side to this search for healing within the family? With patience and faith, loss can build a family; can make it stronger than ever before. A tragic loss is often the catalyst to repair, mend, and enrich family relationships.

The loss of a child may tear a family apart or may cement it forever. A close family will remain close, and may even grow closer as a result of living through this shared horror. Distant family members may discover a new desire to bring relatives together. And the death of a beloved child may create the impetus to work through some marital problems that would have continued to be ignored. "Ken and I are closer than ever." Sarah was beginning to see that even her tragedy had its redemptive side. "We appreciate the good things more than we did and somehow, the little aggravations of daily life don't seem to bother us as they once did. We both try to put things into perspective and focus on what is good, rather than on what is missing. We don't always succeed, but our memories of Jeremy have created an awareness that we never had before." Her husband, Ken, echoed these sentiments, "We realized that we would either survive or drown in our sorrow. We began to really listen to each other. I think we have come to find new respect for each other."

"Our family has been changed forever." That is what it feels like when a child dies. An integral part of us has been transformed from a living participant to a treasured memory. Our time of mourning may also be a time of discovery and growth for those of us who are willing to work at it. No one would ever be so insensitive as to ignore the tragic consequences of a child's death, but even the worst of tragedies can serve to bind the survivors closer to one another. It makes them want to appreciate each other while they can. Family members can no longer take each other for granted. The challenge now is to spend more time together, to try to communicate better.

Deep down, we all know that there is no such thing as certainty. We have no assurance of what tomorrow will bring, but we know that the steps we take today to bind the wounds and to create better family communication will help us on the long journey we are beginning.

13. *Mourning Out of Control*

G rief is invariably complicated because it involves not only a loss, but an attack upon ourselves. When we lose a child, we are, in a sense, losing our future—a part of ourselves. We who have had to live through the emotional roller coaster of grief begin to question ourselves in the most basic ways. We sometimes question our judgment, even our sanity.

It would be a rare parent who has never expressed the worry or asked the question, "Am I going crazy?" The feelings are so strange and foreign that we wonder if anyone else has ever gone through what we are enduring. It is somewhat reassuring to know that these feelings and thoughts are not only "normal", but at some time have been shared by most bereaved parents.

Actually, it is ludicrous to even use the term "normal" when speaking of the death of a child. The death of any child is outside of the realm of what is normal. What could possibly be normal about a child predeceasing a parent? What could be normal about helplessly watching our son or daughter die? But are there patterns that we should question, patterns that send out warning signals? Even allowing for a loose definition of normal, there are certain behaviors that are problematic, and, if these patterns are left untreated, they have the potential to become quite serious.

We have emphasized that there are no timetables, and that all parents will grieve according to an internal, nonspecific, unplanned time schedule that neither they nor anyone else can control. When a child dies, we should not even talk about "extended" or "excessive" mourning until years have passed. We would never attempt to influence a parent's individual mourning style. On the contrary, it is when we see parents who are *not* mourning, that we become concerned.

Failing to grieve may result from any number of factors. When there were ambivalent feelings in our relationship, we often find it difficult to mourn. This might occur when there had been an on-again, off-again relationship between the parents and the child. It might occur when the relationship had been strained, or when problems were not resolved before the child's death. We have seen situations in which parents love their child, but do not like him. A highly ambivalent relationship interferes with the ability to fully grieve because energy that would normally be expended in mourning is diverted into anger and guilt. The anger and guilt are so difficult to handle that one way to deal with them is to walk away from the problem, even to deny its existence.

An inability to grieve may also occur when parents have become too dependent upon their child. Some parents have come to derive an enormous amount of strength from their child, and when death takes away their source of support, their feelings of competency and self-esteem are shaken. They have gradually learned to rely so heavily upon their child that they have lost even minimal confidence in themselves. Their identity has become submerged in the child, who is now gone. For these parents, dealing with their child's death would require opening up all of their feelings about themselves and about their own inadequacies. It may be more than they can emotionally handle. They choose, subconsciously, to just deny what has happened.

Another factor that may create troublesome patterns of mourning may be hidden in the history of the death itself. It is extremely difficult to grieve when the manner or certainty of our child's death is in doubt. A child who is missing, or has been in an accident where there are no identifiable remains — these are situations in which it may be extremely difficult to mourn. In some of these cases, there will never be positive proof of the child's death.

Ed and Helen stared blankly into a room of mourning parents. "She is gone, but..." and here Helen's voice trailed off, "but I just don't know." Ed and Helen's daughter had been a student in China when a ferry sank with 250 lives lost. They knew that Sally was on the boat, but her body was never recovered. For them, the process of mourning was not only excruciating, it was eternal. Even the most unrealistic of hopes prevents us from giving up all hope.

In truth, it is often easier to deny than to deal with tragedy. How often we have read about terrible accidents—a plane crash or a fire in which more than one child is killed, more than one young life being taken before its time. Relatives and friends find it almost impossible to confront the fact that someone they loved so much could be among the victims. When the feelings remain unresolved for years, inevitable problems fester.

Parents who have a history of depressive illness may be expected to have more complicated grief reactions. How they dealt with earlier losses proves to be a clue in understanding these reactions. If a parent had an extremely difficult time dealing with the loss of an uncle, grandmother, or his own parent, it can be anticipated that the loss of their child will be extreme. The resurgence of the memories of those prior losses,

added to an inability to handle grief, exacerbates the
pain and may cause far-reaching complications.

Some people are not able to handle grief at all and
the death of their child becomes doubly difficult. But
we have seen parents, too, whose inability to mourn
dooms them to retreat into themselves even more
deeply. They can not mourn for their relatives or
friends, even for their own parents. And now, their
child has died — and that loss becomes a symbol of all
the frustration and hurt bottled up throughout the
years. Their grief over the loss of their child is
magnified and becomes a metaphor for all the losses
they have endured.

We know that personality differences are expected
factors in dealing with sadness. But sometimes these
differences are so pronounced they lead to family
dysfunction. Such failure to function in a useful way
may be found among those whose grief is just too
intense and difficult to deal with. Escaping into work
or social activities is a common way to avoid facing
grief. As understandable as such reactions are, they
can lead to self-destructive behaviors when carried to
extremes.

Julie was feeling frustrated as she tried once again
to express her anger with the doctors who had
promised her that her daughter, Elizabeth, would be
all right. Elizabeth's fall from a horse had seemed to be
such a minor injury. Everything seemed so positive.
Even after many months, Julie could not believe that
Elizabeth had died. "I run from morning to night"

Julie said, "until I am so tired that all I can do is get some sleep for a few hours. I can't stand being in the house—all those memories." Julie's sleeplessness led to a severe depression and ultimately to hospitalization. A few days after she had expressed her frustration, Julie's car was involved in an accident on a high-speed expressway. She was severely injured. We will never know whether Julie's accident was the result of the trucker's negligence, or from her own exhaustion. Her inability to come to terms with her own grief had severe consequences.

Sometimes the very structure of a family can create problems. We like to think of a family as supportive and nurturing. But what if we are unable to cope with the changes that occur after a tragic loss? We all have a role that we have been given by our families or that we have chosen for ourselves. Whether our role is that of the weak helpless father or the strong capable mother, forcing ourselves to live up to that role while enduring the loss of a child is difficult, and exhsuating. These expectations can interfere with our ability to grieve.

It is when our grief and our roles collide that problems occur. The strong person cannot always feel like being strong while living through something that calls all values and meaning into question. Conversely, a weak member of the family may be compelled by circumstances to act in an entirely new and responsible manner. When our previous roles become forever changed, when they prevent us from acknowledging our true feelings, problems are created. By remaining locked into these predetermined roles, we deny the parts of ourselves that need to be taken care of and allowed to mourn.

But what of the larger world around us? What role does it play? Social factors surely play a part in how parents will grieve. We are all part of that larger world around us, and subject to its influence. Society can be cruel in its judgments. Deaths resulting from an illness or accident are generally regarded as "socially acceptable" deaths, but there are other types of deaths that are not. These may include suicide, AIDS, and drug-related deaths. How many families have felt constrained to remain silent for fear of being embarrassed by a judgmental society? Such avoidance may prove to be quite destructive to members of the family who need to spend much time talking about their loss. Not only may they withdraw, but their inability to share their sadness with others may create a ripple effect within the family.

A strong support network has helped countless parents cope with their grief. Most of us feel that we couldn't have gotten through the long bereavement period without our friends and families. No one can underestimate the importance of this type of support. We would find it hard to go on without the strength and support of others around us. "I never would have made it if it weren't for my friends (parents, brother, etc.)."

But what if we don't have a support system? When we have to face our loss alone, the lack of that additional support complicates our grieving in profound ways. "I felt like I was out in the ocean alone on a sinking ship." William, whose divorce had just been finalized, was giving voice to his loneliness as he sought to understand Jill's tragic accident. "I had no one to talk to, no one I thought would understand. There were nights when I thought the silence would drive me crazy. Even when I was with people, like at work, I still felt all alone in the world. I have never felt so lonely."

Grieving is so complicated that we have to be careful when we label something as an "extended" or "abnormal" grieving process. If there are so many complications to grieving, what then may we regard as extended or abnormal? We may feel that we are acting in ways that are abnormal when what we are doing may be perfectly normal.

Usually, grief is accompanied by constant change. Feelings and emotions ebb and flow. We do not sustain the same level of feelings at all times. Tiny changes take place that we are unaware of on a daily basis. However, grieving parents can look back over six months or a year, and know that they are not the same.

Let us look, then, at some grief reactions that may indicate a need for further help. We agree with William Worden, who classified these reactions into four categories: chronic, delayed, exaggerated, or masked.

A <u>chronic</u> reaction is one in which the mourner does not move through the grief process at all. The chronic mourner is stuck at a point where nothing is changing. There is no relief from the unmitigated pain. Weeks and months and even years pass and there is no growth. If after years of mourning, we are not able to resume a life that allows us to find meaning in our own lives and to relate meaningfully to others, there are unresolved grief issues that need tending. It is not a question merely of time, but of growth.

In <u>delayed</u> grief reactions, the parent may have begun to grieve, but the grieving process is short-circuited because something else must be attended to. The illness of another family member is one such distraction. Energy has to be taken from the act of grieving and focused someplace new. Eventually, however, the sadness has to resurface, even more intensely. Perhaps another death strikes the family and old reactions become inappropriate. Even fictional deaths, stories we may read or watch in a movie, may awaken excruciating memories of unresolved conflicts. Years after the death of their child, a parent may watch a television program in which a child dies. It would be natural for anyone to react sadly, but for a parent whose own mourning feelings have not been resolved, the reaction might well be traumatic. It is the intensity and duration of these reactions that are signals of concern — signals calling for outside intervention and help.

It is natural to be anxious following the death of a child, but when this anxiety turns into a phobia, the feelings may be those of **exaggerated** grief. It is hard to regard mourning the death of a child as something that could be exaggerated. Yet, we have to be aware that when our reaction to loss leads to unrealistic or undiminished anguish, these feelings need to be addressed in a timely manner. There are, for instance, parents who believe they are developing the same symptoms their child had when he was ill. It is not unusual for parents to wish they could have died rather than the child, but when the feeling that they deserve to die along with their child persists, there is reason for concern. A feeling of helplessness is common when mourning a child. Again, these feelings become a problem when mothers or fathers begin to feel that they are unable to go on living without their child.

<u>Masked</u> grief is a form of grief hidden by other feelings. Masked grief occurs when parents act in a way that is troubling to themselves, but they do not make the connection between this behavior and the grief that they are experiencing. Masked grief can manifest itself as pain, illness, or inappropriate behavior.

The story of a father in one of our groups, who was chronically ill, was, in reality, a story of masked grief. John was convinced that he was sick. He went from doctor to doctor and no one could find a thing wrong with him. He refused to make the connection between his inability to mourn and his physical illness. In actuality, his pain was his way of punishing himself. He was content to let himself undergo a life sentence of ill health rather than experience the painful, and in reality, much healthier form of mourning his daughter. Of course, real illness is not to be ignored, nor is it unusual for a real illness to accompany the death of a child. But in the case where the symptoms are chronic and not related to any reality, we need to look to masked grief as a possible source.

What are the warning signals of complicated grief? First, all of these mourning reactions may be "normal" in their own time. They are a concern when they persist, and they are a concern when they do not let us live our lives in a fruitful and creative way. Here are some of them:

1. Inability to speak of our deceased child without an overwhelming emotional sense of sadness that occurs with the same intensity experienced at the very moment of loss. An intense reaction may be triggered by a minor incident, hearing a song on the radio, for example.

2. Inability to touch our child's room or a determination to preserve it exactly as it was at the time of his death. When the room is turned into a shrine, instead of a place of memory, there may well be

a problem. If anyone touches anything, we may become enraged or frantic. If anything that belonged to our child is moved, let alone lost, panic ensues.

3. The manifestation of physical symptoms similar to those experienced by our deceased child, occurring particularly around the anniversary of their death or around any other significant event. The repetitive presence of these symptoms is a signal that something should be re-addressed.

4. Excluding people or things from life because they were part of our child's life. "Her friends want to come and visit, but I can't stand seeing them. It is too upsetting for me." That is how Nancy explained her repeated rejection of her daughter's friends who wished to visit her. "Now I am being invited to showers for her friends who are getting married, and I just can't go. Next thing I know they'll be having babies, and I know I can't bear to watch that. It just isn't fair — Lisa should be with them."

5. Any extremes of emotion. We recognize these emotions as extreme because they prevent us from functioning to the full extent of our abilities. Prolonged and inappropriate euphoria, debilitating depression, or an extreme lack of confidence, low self-esteem and extreme guilt may all be cause for concern.

Imitation may be a way of holding on to a departed child in an attempt not to lose him totally. Brothers or sisters may use imitation to gain the favor of a parent. A few months after his brother's death, Josh suddenly developed a pattern that was not natural for him. He had begun to mimic his brother's unique sense of humor, and that sense of humor was definitely not his own. He would make a joke and look around to see how people reacted. He developed a strange laugh—an unsettling laugh. Josh was trying to become his brother.

Most alarming of all post-death reactions is the contemplation of suicide. Any tendencies toward self-destruction should be taken seriously. Although it is common for parents to want to change places with their dead child, or even wish they were dead, it is quite another thing to plan or attempt a suicide. People may, at times of terrible sadness contemplate their own death in order to escape unbearable pain. But when these thoughts persist or are accompanied by specific plans, a dangerous barrier has been passed. The warning signs should be heeded. Any suicidal thoughts or gestures must always be taken seriously. The old adage "Better to be safe than sorry" certainly holds true here.

Certain times of the year find us particularly vulnerable to our emotions. Holidays and anniversaries are especially dangerous times. Extreme sadness around the time of holidays, birthdays, or the anniversary of a child's death, particularly when these moods are persistent, may be signs of unresolved issues. "Extreme" is the important word here, because parents invariably have a difficult time as special days approach. Sometimes the anticipation is worse than the reality. Sometimes parents can feel upset for days and even weeks before a sad anniversary occurs. This is not at all unusual. What is unusual is when the intensity is such that the parent feels he is reliving the death again, and becomes unable to function in a meaningful way.

And what of parents who seem to enjoy mourning? It may seem ridiculous, but there are instances in which it is possible to make a profession out of their mourning. In these cases, parents have become comfortable as mourners for so long, that any other role seems unreal. Being a mourning parent has, after all, created a role that engenders much sympathy and attention.

Healthy bereaved parents are sad and are capable of feeling for others when they hear a story of another child's death. They can empathize, because they, of all people, know what the newly bereaved parents are facing. On the contrary, parents who are grieving unhealthily may hear a story of another child's death and immediately reframe the story in order to make their own child's death seem more devastating. They yearn to keep the attention on themselves.

How is this done? One way is to diminish the death of others. "Well, at least he lived until he graduated. My son was such a good student and never even got to finish school. He would have been a wonderful doctor." These parents have subconsciously become so used to being in the spotlight, it is difficult for them to relinquish it. It is impossible for them to admit that everyone has problems, and they are a part of a much bigger world than themselves.

These are some of the more common signs that indicate a need for professional help. Of course, friends and family are our first line of support. But, no matter how supportive they are, they are not always equipped to provide the required help. Sometimes the best thing they can do for bereaved parents is to help them find the best professional support possible.

We do not have to suffer helplessly. Individual, couple, and family counseling are available. Sometimes this involves in-depth, repetitive discussions of the tragedy, the experiences that preceded it, and all of the events, feelings, and emotions since. So many parents need to tell and retell their stories. There is only so much of this retelling that can be done with family members or friends. Counseling is a safe place where all of the feelings and emotions can be explored as much as necessary until they can be resolved.

Group counseling or support groups are invaluable in that they give us a chance to talk to other parents who are experiencing feelings similar to our own. There is nothing as comfortable as being in a situation in which we feel understood and accepted, without explaining why we feel so uniquely sad.

Meeting other bereaved parents on a regular basis not only provides a safe haven for expression of emotions, thoughts, and yearnings, but also may help to deal with some of the excesses that often shackle us. But like all things, spending time with other bereaved parents can be overdone. Rejecting old friends and **only** wanting to spend time with other parents who have lost children limits our opportunities for growth.

A support group is most useful when it provides opportunities for mutual sharing while avoiding the temptation to become an end in itself. It is important for leaders of these groups to remember the warning of Ecclesiastes: "There is a time to weep" but also "there is a time to laugh" (Ecc. 3:4). Yes, sometimes there is a time to laugh, beyond the sadness, beyond the anguish, beyond the pain... there is a time to laugh too.

Obviously, excessive use of alcohol, drugs or sedatives are warning flags. A physician may prescribe sedatives, but too much reliance on these, as well as other less healthy escape hatches should be carefully watched. Here is a scenario we have seen all too often. A distraught parent seeks medical assistance. The doctor, feeling helpless in the face of such deep sadness prescribes antidepressants. Their overuse can become a crutch or an even more serious impediment to the necessary grieving process.

It took years for George to realize that his alcoholism not only lead to the destruction of his family but was, in a sense, a form of suicide. He still was uncomfortable talking about it. "I could work all day, but the moment I entered the house, I needed to be insulated from the pain. So I drank, and I drank, and I drank until I fell asleep." Fortunately, George recognized his addiction and by attending both Alcoholics Anonymous meetings and a parental support group, he was able to salvage his life and begin a new family.

Although opinions differ on the advisability of medication aimed solely at removing the pain of mourning, our general belief is that it is best to deal with grief as much as possible without this kind of aid. Mourning is real and painful. Medications may dull the senses. They often make it seem as if the pain has been dispelled. But it is not gone. The only way to get through the pain is to live through it and feel it. Taking medication unnecessarily will only prolong an admittedly lengthy process. It will not shorten the process.

There are, of course, times when medication is warranted. If we are unable to sleep, medications may help on a short-term basis. But we have to recognize that sleeplessness is as much a part of grief as prolonged periods of sleep may be. As parents, we need to be able to get some rest in order to function. Without it, we may begin a destructive spiral of exhaustion. But, prolonged sleeplessness cannot be treated with pills.

We all feel abnormal at times. We all feel that we are "crazy" or at risk of "going crazy." These feelings add to the already scary and overwhelming problems bereaved parents have to deal with. One evening, Jan came to our parents' meeting acting distraught. She had lost her car keys and had become obsessed by her memory lapse. "All of this has happened since Karen died. I felt so stupid. I don't do things like that. I feel like I am losing my mind."

We all know that it is not a great tragedy to lose one's car keys. What is sad is when these memory lapses become so overwhelming they cause us to relive the far greater tragedy that has befallen us and to question our capabilities—even our worth. As we all know, this could happen to anyone, bereaved or not. As mourning people, we are constantly trying to check to see if we are still the people we once were. Any simple incident may hamper our coping skills and leave us feeling as if we are losing our minds. When this pattern occurs frequently, or when it paralyzes our judgment, it is time to turn to others for help. The difference between normalcy and pathology may be a fine line. The distinction must be carefully examined, not in times of panic or momentary distress, but with a goal of long-term growth.

14. The Search for Faith

"Oh God, I want to see my son some day." This simple cry sums up a thousand prayers of mourning parents. It also lies at the heart of hundreds of theologies. Essential to so many religions is the desire to explain the most profound mystery of all — what happens to us after we die. Though the answers may vary, almost every belief system seeks to offer comfort and the hope that death is not the end.

Each of us comes to view the afterlife through the eyes of our religious or family belief systems. We may be able to accept those traditions with total faith, or we may rebel against them, but we cannot fail to be impressed by the durability of some basic themes that keep occurring over and over in our ongoing search for comfort. Life teaches us in ways that lead us either to accept or to deny these traditions. But all these different ways of viewing what happens when we die do not affect the hope that seems to transcend religious and spiritual boundaries: "I want to see my son...I want to see my daughter...some day."

This simple entreaty, however, is but a primal call to faith in its most elemental form. Behind it are the affirmations as well as the doubts that parents have expressed through the centuries. When we lose a child, we so often become the victims of our anger — anger at a husband or wife, anger at a doctor, even occasionally at the child who has been taken from us. Of all the rage we experience, none may be more bitter than our anger toward God. "How could a loving and kind God do this to me?" Even the rage of a betrayed husband or wife could not be more bitter. After a lifetime of trust, how could that God of justice and loving-kindness allow this terrible injustice? The angry question can be seen as an affirmation and accusation. After all, the very anger we feel is based upon the fact that we believe. We cannot be angry with someone who does not exist.

When we lose a child we often are forced to the edge of faith. Will we fall over the edge and allow a lifetime of belief to come crashing after us, or can we retreat from the spiritual chasm that yawns before us and draw strength from the tradition of which we are a part? Whatever religion we choose to accept, we have to recognize that it has led other parents through that dark "valley of the shadow of death" in the past, and it will do so again. We are not the first to tread that bleak path, even as we know we will not be the last.

Throughout the centuries our religious traditions have become quite aware of the complexities of human life. The questions they raise and even the consolation they offer, may sometimes seem confusing and even contradictory and yet they are sources of tremendous strength. Some of us want simple answers and expect our faith to cast a light for us as we haltingly seek comfort. We have discovered that the answers are seldom simple, that different people will find help in diverse ways, and sometimes in the most unexpected quarters. The point of this chapter is to reveal the help found in the age-old ideas that permeate our religious traditions. We can benefit from that help if we are patient enough to look for it and accept it when it is accessible.

"I cannot believe in an afterlife. It is all over." We hear these words too, and more than occasionally. Just as some of us depend upon our faith to help us through the rough places of our lives, there are those who deny something beyond the boundaries of this mortal span. Does it mean that these people lack faith? The question put in this way is not especially useful. The question should be, Does this form of rationalism offer comfort? And for some people it does. Some people can only believe the evidences of their eyes and their ears and their minds. They are not interested in envisioning anything beyond the empirical view they have of this earth. Is this a religious belief? For many people it is. If God's role is merely to create the universe, and then leave it alone, as many naturalists believe, then there can be no expectation of any comforting role for either God or religion. For them, the belief that God's role is not that of a comforter is in itself a source of consolation. Of course this view of God may leave many of us feeling empty and unanswered.

Most major religions have more than a single view of what happens to us after we die. Even the most fundamental faiths admit more than one vision of the afterlife. This may seem like heresy to those who believe that there is only one true faith. But most of our historic religions have welcomed commentators who interpreted the divine word and the divine text in new and innovative ways. Buddhism, Judaism, Christianity, Islam, Hinduism — they have all been studied and explained by scores of scholars and saints and rabbis who sought answers to the same problems that trouble us today. In addition, the very survival of those religions that have stood the test of time invites a process in which ideas are molded and modified over centuries.

Not surprisingly, most of what we can say about an afterlife is grounded in a belief that goes back thousands of years. Well-entrenched patterns of belief are often challenged when they come up against the reality of a loss. So many parents have simply said, "I cannot believe any more. I cannot believe in God. I cannot believe in anything." But there is no time when belief is more desperately needed than when we lose a child. And there is no time when a faith, even a faith we question, can be more helpful.

We are going to try to study some of these belief patterns to see if they can help us in a significant way, but first we have to understand one important thought. We cannot help one another or ourselves if we insist on picturing the end of our journey as one of hopeless interminable suffering. We have to assert this thought, because newly bereaved parents are often caught in a mental quicksand, which leaves them feeling not only unable, but also unwilling to break free of their anguish. Here is their problem. They simultaneously want to be comforted and to resist being comforted. And here is why. The very act of feeling comforted appears to be an act of betrayal to the memory of the child they loved so much. How can I feel happy since I have just lost my child? The minute many parents begin to feel better they have to feel worse — and the cycle seems impossible to break. Although the death of a child creates an irrevocable and traumatic agony, the path that each parent takes can indeed end not in despair, but in renewal.

Throughout the centuries our religions have sought to help us find this path to renewal. They help us by encouraging us to think about faith as something much more than a doctrine, but rather as a very comforting guide along the road we travel.

We are going to take a look at these guides and try to divide them into a few helpful categories. But first, a word of warning: It would be easy to say, "This is what Judaism believes. This is what Christianity or Islam believes." While it is important to understand the doctrines our major religions hold, when it comes to death and mourning, we feel that a classification along structural denominational lines can often be misleading. Such a classification is often too simple. Most major religions, as we have suggested, have more than one explanation of what happens after we die. It becomes a task too technical for this book to do justice to the nuances and variations that proliferate in our various religions. But it can be helpful to divide the historical ideas about an afterlife into a few categories.

Resurrection

There will come a time when we will all be together again. Those who have died will come back to life. Believers in resurrection comprise two distinct categories: those who believe the body and soul will be reunited at some future place and time, and those who believe that the soul alone will attain a new physical form that will allow it to persist throughout the ages. A messiah or divine personality will precipitate the resurrection. This messianic figure may be the Son of God or one chosen by God. For some religions, resurrection will take place in time and space. That means there will be a specific place to which the dead will return. Since a physical resurrection will occur, we bury our dear ones as soon as possible, and do not disturb their bodies. Embalming and cremation are forbidden since these practices make it more difficult, though not always impossible, for the resurrection to occur.

For those religious people who believe that the soul will attain some resurrected form, the return to life will take place not on this earth but in heaven. This resurrection will not involve our bodies, but only our souls. Not space, but time is the crucial element. The rebirth will take place in a world beyond our world, one we cannot see, but only imagine. Since all of us are made up of body and soul, the body may die, but the soul will enjoy a rebirth at a dramatic moment in time.

Inherent in all resurrection doctrines is the belief that death here on earth does not signal the end of our existence. For the righteous, at least, there is the faith that the best is yet to come. So many people find a belief in resurrection comforting because it offers hope that in the future, even if it is a distant one, we will be united with those we love.

Immortality of the soul

Like many doctrines of resurrection, belief in the immortality of the soul holds that there is a clear distinction between the body and the soul. It is the soul and not the body that will live on after we have died. Instead of facing a rebirth, our souls live on in some perfect or heavenly place where they remain in perfect union with God. They continue to bless and inspire those who live on after them, and they may be able to act as intercessors or advocates before God on behalf of those left behind on earth. Many parents find comfort in feeling that their child is with God. How paradoxical it is that what some parents find comforting on this score proves to be unsettling to others. "God wanted my daughter." "She is with God." How starkly these words stand against the cry we hear so often: "How could God do this to me?" Those who believe in the immortality of the soul find comfort in the knowledge that death is not an ending, but rather the beginning of a new form of existence.

Transmigration

The idea that the body is merely a home to be inhabited for a while is essential to the doctrine of transmigration. The real essence of being is the soul. It lives on until it finds release from its journey through life. Human beings are destined to return to this world, but not in the body in its present form. The soul will return in another form. It will migrate from body to body to body, and the life the soul takes will be more desirable than the one we have left. Death does not mark the end of the voyage, but merely a stage in the journey. Resignation is better than selfishness. To resist death is a form of selfishness and pride. Death is a universal heritage, and it is best accepted with equanimity. The belief in the transmigration of souls can provide great comfort to those who believe in the cyclical nature of human existence and in the permanence of the creative process.

Death as a lesson in life

Inherent in most religions is a feeling that each life has a lesson to teach. Those who die bless us through the lives they lived. Their immortality consists of the good deeds they performed. This doctrine can be seen as standing against the traditional ideas of resurrection, immortality, or transmigration in that none of these traditional ideas is necessary to believe that the death of someone we love has a lesson to teach. Most faiths do believe that in addition to what they have to say about an afterlife, those we love do leave something with us that blesses and inspires us. Even the death of a child — especially the death of a child — has a lesson to teach. We know the meaning of love in a new way. We can share that lesson and, in turn, pass it on to others as our own heritage. We can do this as a result of all we have suffered and learned.

Of course, no summary as brief as this one can do justice to the rich complexity that our historic religious ideas incorporate. And of course, at a time of anguish, theological doctrine may be the last thing we want to hear. All we know is that we are in pain, and quick fixes are the things we reject most quickly. In a time of suffering, we all recognize that faith is not an easy thing to grasp. There are so many moments when we are too depressed to even listen to what our faith has to offer. There are moments when we are resentful. There are moments when we are furious. These feelings and moods are perfectly appropriate, even necessary. But they have their time, they have their season — and so does healing have its season.

Sooner or later, all of us who lose a child need to make a crucial decision. Can we get out of bed in the morning? The question is, of course, a metaphor for saying yes to life. How often we hear parents literally give a negative answer to this question. "I don't even want to get out of bed in the morning. I can't face life." We have to ask ourselves the question in an affirming way. Can we turn from despair and face the future? Can we realize that there is other suffering and other sadness that is as legitimate as our own? These questions have even more serious overtones. Will we allow our loss to destroy us along with our child?

Here is where a well-practiced faith can help us. It can call us toward others. Religious doctrines are, of course, useful, but they are useful only as they pull us away from our bitterness.

The agony that King David had to endure is one example of a parent living through a time of anguish. David's son had become critically ill. David prayed for the child. He fasted. No one could get him to move, no one could get him to talk — so devastated was he. And, after seven days, the child died. Everyone around King David was afraid to tell him the news. "When the child was alive," they reasoned, "David refused to talk. What will the king be like now that his son is dead?"

David saw them whispering. "Is my son dead?" he asked. And they said, "He is dead." And then David rose up from his place of mourning. He bathed and anointed himself, and went to the house of God to pray. "What is this thing you have done?" they asked. "While your son was alive, you fasted and wept. But as soon as he died you got up and you ate bread." David answered his servants with these words: "While the child was alive, I fasted and wept. Who knows whether I could not have kept him alive. But now that he is dead, why should I fast? Can I bring him back again? I shall go to him, but he will not return to me."

King David's example is a hard one to follow, but there is wisdom in this old biblical story. Our greatest challenge is to bless the living. Can we not find some comfort in resolving both guilt and regret and discovering that we really had done all that we could while our son or daughter was still alive? And is there not wisdom in realizing that there is a time to get on with our lives, a time to turn toward the future?

Sooner or later our feelings of guilt and bitterness need to be replaced by a sense of purpose. Our children are best remembered not by bitterness, but by love. All of the feelings we have for our children are desecrated if they ultimately leave us only with anger and resentment.

A parent in one of our groups asked an important and helpful question. Some of her daughter's friends had asked her to join them at a party. She didn't feel comfortable saying yes, and she felt equally uncomfortable rejecting their act of kindness. And so she asked this question: "What would Lisa want me to do?" A question like this can be helpful in so many ways. What would Lisa want me to do? Not only can this question lead us to a comfortable answer to a real dilemma, it can also help us to redefine our attitudes toward life itself.

Of course our deceased children cannot dictate solutions to our current life problems. These solutions must be found in the living context of our daily lives. But the values we have taught our children live on even when our children are gone. In a very true sense, our children really do teach us, just as we once taught them. What would my daughter want me to do? What would my son want me to do? We have not created in vain, nor have we lost everything. Our children can still guide and bless us just as we tried to guide and bless them.

Would my daughter want me to be sad for the rest of my life? The question demands an answer. The answer will not depend upon her age at the time of her death. It depends upon a relationship that is timeless. Would my son want me to be sad for the rest of my life? This question raises again the problem we have asked so often: How can I distinguish between a mourning process that expresses sadness and yearning, and one that destroys and embitters my life? Ultimately this distinction is one that can be resolved by no doctrine, by no clergy or physician. It is a question that we ourselves must honestly confront.

Would my daughter want me to miss her and think of her often in loving and life-giving ways, or would she want me to dwell in a world of tears and perpetual misery? Would she want me to go on with my life and lend my talents to good people and good causes, or would she want me to spend my days in unremitting bitterness?

The search for faith leads us along many different paths. As we have seen, what may be comforting to one person can be profoundly disturbing to another. A cemetery is an example of how different people react to different symbols. For some parents, the cemetery is a painful reminder of everything they want to avoid. For others, returning to the cemetery represents a return to the place where they last visited with the physical remains of their child. Many people find this act of homage profoundly comforting. George Burns, who lived until he was almost 100 years old, used to tell of how he would go to his wife's grave every day during those first years after she had died. "I needed to talk things over with Gracie," he said.

Many of us feel that the cemetery is the place where we can still "talk things over" with the one we miss so much. It is also the place where the connection between the living and the dead can be most palpably experienced. Standing at the grave of our child, regardless of whether such an experience means that we can speak to our child or merely be at the place where we last did something for our child, represents an opportunity for us to combine the physical and spiritual sides of our mourning and to allow faith to point us toward our future.

To find hope, to find faith, to find the way we can turn our sadness into service for others, and into love in our own lives—this is the greatest challenge of loss. It is also the greatest opportunity.

15. The Awesome Revelation
How Can I Face the Future Without my Child?

The people sit around the room. They sit in a semicircle and stare silently at one another. No one wants to start the conversation. They sit in silence, mothers and fathers who have lost a child. And then they start to talk, to tell their stories-- sometimes, unbearable stories: A son who fell and was strangled as he tried to climb into his locked home after school. A daughter who was murdered by her enraged father, who could not face the divorce suit that his wife was about to bring against him. A college daughter killed as she begged her college date to drive more slowly after a fraternity party. The boy was not injured, not even a scratch.

The parents face one another in a semicircle and gradually find comfort only in the realization that there are others, too, who have lost; others, too, who feel the aching, unending pain. "When will it end?"

one mother finally asks. "When will the pain end?" "Never" is the answer, uttered more with certainty than with hopelessness. "It will never end."

The answer, however, is not so simple. The pain will change. Like all human feelings, it will grow and wane, focus and dim. It never leaves; rather, it transforms itself until it has a life of its own. This pain for the loss of our children does indeed have a life of its own, just as real, in a way, as were the lives of our children themselves. That the pain never ends does not mean that its sharpness is untouched by time. Indeed, time does dull the sting, but in ways that do more to transform than to diminish.

The truth is—the child we have lost is always a part of our thoughts and dreams. The truth is--our child is fixed in living images that never die. Our child never grows older. Our fifteen-year-old son will always be a fifteen-year-old. We may imagine what he would be like now, but in reality, he will always be fifteen years old. For other parents who watched their twenty-nine-year-old daughter die while giving birth to a child, there would always be a presence of another kind. The grandchild who survived would grow and flourish. Her grandmother might well watch her approach, and then pass, the age of her own daughter when she died. Gradually their lives might even merge into one another's and the mourning parent would watch her granddaughter add year to year while her daughter would remain immortally young. "Perhaps in her mind the pain changes," the parents will say, but it never disappears. To let it disappear would be unimaginable, as we have seen. To let it disappear would be to forget, and what parent is willing to forget a beloved child?

Parents who have lost are willing to indulge behavior in themselves that they would not have tolerated previously. They develop taboos and fixations that may seem irrational to others. They are not immune to contradictions in their own behavior. They are drawn to places and repelled by places-- places that remind them of their children, places that symbolize the love and the anguish that remind them of their loss. They may dread holidays and anniversaries, for example, yet would not let them pass unnoticed, for they arouse sacred memories.

The eccentricities of place are particularly poignant. "Sam and I used to take this walk in a woods near our house," one father noted. "Now, whenever I want to feel better about Sam's death, I take this walk with him. And we talk...only Sam is not there."

But places, too, can become a burden upon our memories. It was William who was talking. William remembered that terrible train accident that took his college-age daughter from him. William used to run a camp in the summer. He remembered how after his divorce he would take his daughter with him to camp every year. "I never really appreciated her enough. We were always so busy checking on counselors, checking on menus for dinner, checking on campers smoking pot after hours. But Jill was always there. I knew it, and I loved it. Then she died. I couldn't face things any more. I got rid of the camp as quickly as I could. I can't go there again. Never again."

Patterns of attraction and avoidance may well be layered with sentiments that in reality have little to do with the child who has died. We often grant ourselves "indulgences." We indulge ourselves when we misuse our sorrow to rationalize our avoidance of an unpleasant task or responsibility. Think of something that you never liked to do. Your reasons may be quite genuine, as, of course, are your feelings for your lost daughter.

An indulgence occurs when we synthetically attach our mourning to those things that have nothing to do with our loss, but are innately distasteful to us. A task you never liked to do or a place you never liked to visit becomes permanently rejected and rationalized. "My memories are too bitter for me to return to that place." These parents are indulging their preferences, attributing to them the sadness they feel, excusing them because "after all, we are mourners." This feeling is often handled with an almost carefree indifference to what others may think. "I have suffered enough. I don't care what anyone else wants me to do."

Unfortunately, these indulgent thoughts may prolong the mourning process. By attaching our mourning to any distasteful task or to any unpleasant place we can easily fall into the trap of misusing our mourning in unhealthy ways. There are responsibilities that we must accept, journeys we must take. We simply have to face the fact that having lost a child does not excuse us from the responsibilities that beckon us.

And yet, there is something we must understand if we are to truly realize the impact of these indulgent tendencies that we often experience. We have to face the reality that so many mourners begin to feel — I have become a different person — different from what I was, and, different from anyone who has not lost a child.

More than one quite sane parent has said it: "I am now a little bit crazy." And what is this feeling about being crazy that so many of us experience? Basically, it is that we are now a different person — and we are not quite able to accept the changes we perceive in ourselves. There are many factors that are part of the new person that we have become. There is the loss itself, which so few of our friends have had to experience. In addition, we may develop an indifference to some of the values that other people hold. This compounds the feeling that "I am a little bit crazy."

"I am now so different that I don't care what anyone else thinks." The expectation of friends and relatives that it is time to stop mourning merely intensifies these feelings of eccentricity. "Everyone wants me to stop mourning." In reality, these expectations meet a cold wall of resistance, and even hostility, from parents who will not be cast in the role of "ordinary mourners."

It is not unusual, therefore, for a certain degree of isolation to occur as we parents proceed along our own stumbling path. There are friends who never seem capable of understanding that we need to follow our own unique timetable, and that healing is a slow and unsteady process.

Do we lack concentration? Have we become absentminded? These are the things that often accompany the growing feeling that we are no longer totally normal. In reality, these mental lapses are the quite ordinary evidences of minds that are overflowing with such painful memories.

Nor is the sequence of our feelings totally predictable. Moments of compassion may be followed by moments of fear, fear by anger, anger by remorse and remorse by compassion again. There is no order to these feelings. All sorts of conflicting thoughts crash and tumble together, but all are part of the ultimately reasonable process of trying to "sort things out", to bring sanity to what no sane person can ever justify or fully explain.

"You will never forget your child," newly bereaved parents sitting around the room are told by other parents. What at first seems upsetting gradually becomes comforting. Who would want to forget? Who would try to forget? Who would erase the memory — so poignant, so important, so totally beautiful? The memory, therefore becomes essential to the return to wholeness, a journey that, while never completed, need not be a hopeless one. "You will be changed," they are told. And they are changed. Some become more bitter, unable to trust again. Some become more compassionate, seeing in every reported loss an echo of their own loss.

What once seemed important is now dismissed as trivial. Conversely, what was once dismissed as a meaningless moment in a parent-child relationship now becomes a cherished memory. Who could have predicted, and who can understand now, why one moment above all others has become a sacred memory?

The task all parents face is whether to become bitter or better. Even that formulation simplifies the dilemma, assuming that our feelings can be separated from one another, categorized as good or bad, healthy or unhealthy. In truth, there are no eternally valid judgments to be made at the time of losing a child. Each parent follows a unique path – and each path is authentic in its own way.

What we have to encourage, however, is the choice of a path that leads us to a constructive, rather than a destructive, expression of our grief. If our grief results in unmitigated bitterness, if there is no awareness of the universal nature of suffering, if there is no effort at least to come to grips with the meaning of our tragedy as well as the possibilities of love, then more than a child has died.

At Gettysburg, President Lincoln prayed that the honored dead "shall not have died in vain." Indeed, he was talking of the children whose bones lay recently interred in that Pennsylvania burial ground. No parent can rest in the bitter assumption that there is no meaning in our children's lives. We need to feel that, despite the shortness of their lives, our children continue to symbolize something eternal, something that will not die. And we need to feel that from our memories of them, unquenchable love still bridges the chasm of space and time.

And so, there comes a time, perhaps after months, perhaps after many years, when we can turn from mourning to other tasks. When this happens, we begin, in new ways, to bring to life the memory of the one we loved so much. The change may begin with the creation of a memorial project or fund that captures the essence of our child. It may begin with the dedication of a playground for little children the age of our child. It may begin with adopting a baby rejected by an unwed mother. Or it may begin by being able to come to a meeting of bereaved parents, and realizing, for the first time, that we have come to give help to others, instead of only needing to take help from them.

Such steps do not just automatically occur. The healing we experience may, at first, be quite imperceptible. It is often preceded by a dawning realization that our world is filled with mystery. The mystery touches at the meaning of life itself. We cannot explain everything; we cannot pretend that the unexpected occurs only to other people. To the extent that accidents happen, they are indeed accidents, unplanned events that offer no explanation, even when they might have been avoided. To wish to undo what has happened is in itself a way of trying to rationalize the tremendous mystery that is the reality of life. For we have yet to understand who will live and who will die, much less how to avoid every volcanic explosion of nature.

In a very real sense, an acknowledgment of this irrationality as it touches so many of the important things of life is the beginning of maturity. Just as we can never quite understand the depth of our love, we can never truly fathom the depth of our anguish when tragedy occurs. We can only learn to appreciate the ultimate possibilities of life and to move forward with unrelenting faith.

"How could God do this to me?" cries the grieving parent. We do not need to adopt the theological view, comforting to some of us, but not to all, that God acts with ultimate wisdom, to understand that maturity lies in our ability to face the future. Faith and reason do not always live in harmony with one another. We may not ever totally understand why tragedy has singled us out—yet, we may seek and find the faith that will allow us to move forward in our lives.

For grieving parents, learning to smile again may be as difficult as learning to walk again. For some, the task must be undertaken step-by-step. For others, the dawn does not occur gradually, but in sudden thrusts of sunlight that break through the darkness of the night. Each parent is an individual, destined to travel a long and lonely path, a path on which no mercenary can be hired to travel as our surrogate.

"Bittersweet" is the word parents use to describe their memories. Bitter—full of anger and remorse, full of "if onlys" and "What might have beens." Sweet—thoughts of our children, thoughts of holidays and birthdays together, thoughts of love and of walking together and talking together.

Beyond all our memories is the realization that there is a task remaining to be done. Memories of our children may evoke resentment and bitterness. Or they may challenge us to rebuild shattered lives, to love even more deeply those who are left to us, and to dedicate ourselves to hopes yet to be envisioned.

An old and wise man, so the story goes, was revered by all who knew him. But two young men could not stand the saintly man's popularity, and vowed to test him. They devised a diabolical plan. They would take a bird, and come before him with the bird in their hands. They would challenge him. "Is the bird dead or alive?" Their plan was to let the bird soar free if he answered "dead", and to crush it in their hands if he answered "alive." Either way, the sage would be humiliated. And so they acted. They found the bird. They took it in their hands. They approached the old man. "Is the bird dead or alive?" they challenged. For a moment, there was silence.

And then the old man replied: "The answer, my friends, is in your hands."

The ultimate truth of his answer is something that must be understood by all of us who mourn and continue to love.

Epilogue: The Elevator

I had gone to visit him just the night before. The lights in his hospital room seemed especially dim. Cradled in his arm was the football that Joe Namath had signed and sent him. He really loved that football, and couldn't stop talking about how nice it was of Joe Namath to send it to him. I sat by his bed that night and listened to his heavy breathing. I reached out for his warm hand and held it in mine for a few minutes.

I remember bending my head over his chest, and suddenly I was crying. I don't know why I did it. I had never wanted him to see me crying. But now I had no control over what was happening. I simply sobbed out, "Oh, my son, how I wish it were me instead of you!"

He put his hands around my head and pressed it to his chest. And he said, "You don't know how good that makes me feel." That was all he said. And then it was time to say goodnight.

In the morning I went to a breakfast meeting with some people who always used to impress me with their achievements. A famous novelist was there. A well-published sociologist. A magazine editor. We were talking about how we could make the world a better place in which to live. We talked about wars and weapons, about poverty and homelessness. We talked about what we had done, about what we could do to change the world to make it better. And then I went to the hospital to see my son.

When I reached the corridor near my son's room, three nurses rushed toward me. Something was different. I sensed it. I knew it. They took me into a conference room. They made me sit down. Your son died. He died an hour ago. He died peacefully. I could not believe it, yet I knew it was true. I went into his room and looked at his closed eyes, his gaunt face, his folded hands. I bent down and kissed him. "I love you," I said. "I love you. I love you."

I was saving the world, and my son was dying! That was the thought that came to me then and echoed through the hours and days that followed.

A kindly nurse held my hand. She gave me a plain paper bag and helped me put my son's things into it – a few shirts, a pair of brown trousers, a pair of pajamas – and the football that Joe Namath had signed. I took the bag and started to walk. I walked out of the hospital, across the park. I didn't care where I was going. I just needed to walk. I was saving the world and my son was dying. There were children playing in the park. I remember that they were there, but hardly remember what they were shouting about or doing. The sun was shining and children were playing in the park. I was saving the world and my son was dying. I noticed those children and I walked on. All I could do was walk.

Hours later, I reached my apartment building and slowly entered through the revolving door. The building was a new one and the elevators were not yet totally reliable. I recognized the well-dressed, middle-aged lady who stood tapping her foot impatiently. "Aren't these elevators the most annoying thing you've seen?" she asked.

The most annoying thing? What is the most annoying thing? I suppose I could have become furious at the foot-tapping lady. Maybe I should have screamed at her. Maybe I should have yelled out: "You don't know what annoying is. You don't know what life is!" So many thoughts rushed through my mind. Angry thoughts. Tearful thoughts. Anguished thoughts.

But something happened to me in that moment that I have never regretted. In the midst of that tremendous sadness, something happened that was not sad. In that moment of thinking about what to say, I realized that no one, no one can ever quite know my pain, and that I can never completely understand the pain of others. But pain is universal. I have come to realize in a new way that every loss is unique, and that loss leaves no one unmarked. I can understand what it means to lose a lifetime partner, or even to lose a beloved pet. They are all losses — real losses. And I can empathize with the pain of others without feeling that I have somehow betrayed the memory of my son — I loved him so much. I like to feel, even now, so many years later, that my son taught me that lesson in compassion — even for that impatient lady waiting for the elevator doors to open.

Yes, perhaps it would have made me feel better to yell. Perhaps I would have been better off if I could have cried. There were plenty of tears later, and I could not, would not take one back. The elevator finally arrived. As I got on it, with a paper bag of memories in my hand, I simply said, "Yes, it is annoying."

Acknowledgements

The creation of this book was the product of years of listening and learning. It would be impossible to thank all of those who made our work possible. It is incumbent on us, however, to acknowledge those most directly responsible for helping us as we embark upon our task. Jane Goldberg and Lois Mandel died before our work was completed. Their help and encouragement were a profound blessing. We are indebted to Al and Sheila Wengerhoff who inspired Susan to devote her life to helping others. Dr. Nan Gitlin and Dr. David Clark were important teachers we encountered along the way. Their knowledge and example were a source of valuable insight. To Brook Noel, our publisher, and to Nancy Rosenfeld, our agent , we are deeply indebted. They saw the potential in our work and made the publication of this a reality. To Marjorie and Richard Marx who lived through the pain of losing a son and brother, and to Ruth Marx who offered constant advice and encouragement, we are lastly grateful. Finally, no words of appreciation can be concluded without our thanking the hundreds of parents who opened their hearts as we listened, and allowed us to travel with them on their painful journey.

To contact the authors, send mail to

Robert J. Marx and/or Susan Wengerhoff Davidson
c/o Champion Press, Ltd.
4308 Blueberry Road
Fredonia, WI 53021

To order additional books, order online at www.championpress.com or send $14.95 for each paperback version, $22.95 for each hardcover to the above address. Please include $3.95 shipping/handling for the first book and $1.00 for each additional book. Wisconsin residents, please add 5.5% sales tax.